HOW TO GET INTO

The Right

MEDICAL

SCHOOL

Carla S. Rogers, Ph.D.

Printed on recyclable paper

VGM Career Horizons
a division of *NTC Publishing Group*
Lincolnwood, Illinois USA

Library of Congress Cataloging-in-Publication Data

Rogers, Carla S.
    How to get into the right medical school / Carla S. Rogers.
        p. cm.
    Includes bibliographical references.
    ISBN 0-8442-4161-X (p: alk. paper).
      1. Medical colleges—United States—Admission. 2. Medicine—
Vocational guidance—United States. I. Title.
    [DNLM: 1. School Admission Criteria. 2. Schools, Medical.
    3. Educational Measurement.   W 18 R724h 1996]
    R838.4.R64   1996
    610'.71'173—dc20
    DNLM/DLC
    for Library of Congress   96-325
                                                    CIP

Published by VGM Career Horizons, a division of NTC Publishing Group
4255 West Touhy Avenue
Lincolnwood (Chicago), Illinois 60646-1975, U.S.A.
©1996 by NTC Publishing Group. All rights reserved.
No part of this book may be reproduced, stored in a retrieval
system, or transmitted in any form or by any means,
electronic, mechanical, photocopying, recording or otherwise,
without the prior permission of NTC Publishing Group.
Manufactured in the United States of America.
6 7 8 9 0 VP 9 8 7 6 5 4 3 2 1

Contents

This book is dedicated to the memory of my father,
Arthur Needham Rogers

Preface

"The future belongs to those who believe in the beauty of their dreams."   *Eleanor Roosevelt*

Have you ever thought about being a doctor? Have you ever wondered about what it takes to become one? Where do you begin? How do you decide whether this is the right career for you? Is medical school really that tough? Where do I go for information? Who can I talk to? Help!

In 1994, nearly 43,000 people applied to medical school. Of all those applicants, only 16,307 entered medical school. And the competition is increasing. In the immediate future, applicants may be competing with more than 60,000 others. With the number of people interested in a medical career skyrocketing, how can you increase your chances of being accepted into a medical school program?

My career in a medical school has encompassed being a professor, researcher, and assistant dean for admissions and student affairs. For many of those years, I was on admissions committees. I have talked to countless high school students, college students, and people interested in making a career change. And they all have similar questions, problems, and fears. Often, during admissions presentations and interviews, I would think, "All these people need some basic information *before* they arrive at this interview step." So this book is written for *you*. *You*, if you are thinking about medicine as a career, if you want to take the Medical College Aptitude Test, if you have always wanted to be a doctor, but lack confidence in yourself. It is for you if you are writing your application at this very moment or if you are currently interviewing, at medical schools. This book is designed to answer your questions. It is written to give you essential advice on how to approach the many areas of the medical school admissions process and how to experience success all along the way.

The best of luck to each and every one of you in your search for a successful, rewarding, and fulfilling medical career.

Acknowledgments

I would first like to thank my husband, Dr. Frank Austin Redmond, for his editing, suggestions, constant encouragement, and for the dinners he cooked while I was writing. I love you.

I would also like to acknowledge my two sons, Christopher and Nicholas, who were always willing to give up their Nintendo playing and computer games while I was working.

Many thanks are extended to Bill Beausay, author and good friend, whose advice I often sought during the past year. And also to Reverend Mark Montgomery and family—I will always be grateful for their support and love.

To Dr. Barry Richardson and Deb Heineman—their knowledge was invaluable.

And thanks Mom, Linda, and Pamela.

Introduction

So You Want to be a Doctor

"Two roads diverged in a wood, and—I took the one less traveled by, And that has made all the difference."   Robert Frost

Ever since you were five years old you've been dreaming about what you want to be when you grow up. You may have dreamed of being a firefighter, a police officer, a pilot, an artist, a teacher, a scientist, an astronaut. Who you wanted to be would change on a weekly basis. Or perhaps you were one of those kids who knew from the very first time you bandaged your younger brother's scraped knee that you wanted to be a doctor, and nothing short of that goal would do.

Whether you have had the dream of becoming a doctor for 15 years or 15 minutes, you have taken the first step. You have chosen your career goal. But so often, the "real world" begins to wreak havoc with our dreams. Financial problems may beset your family. Suddenly your dream of Harvard becomes the reality of your local community college. Death of a parent or sibling, or a debilitating illness in a family member, may force you to work and postpone school. Earning a "C" in organic chemistry may contribute to losing confidence in yourself. Whatever the roadblocks, you need to fight for what you want. Only you can make your dream of becoming a physician come true. First, you must learn *how* to make your dream a reality. You need information about the medical profession and medical schools. You need to create a plan to reach your first goal—getting into medical school. And you need to take action—by constantly learning

...d working towards your goals, by discovering yourself, your skills, and your inner strengths. You must discover in yourself the qualities it takes to become a successful physician.

First of all, do you know what a physician actually does? According to Benjamin H. Natelson, M.D., author of *Tomorrow's Doctors*, most people think that the student who goes to medical school learns how to cure disease. In reality, the number of illnesses and diseases that can be cured with medical treatment is fairly small. Today, certain infections (bacterial, fungal, and some viral) can be cured. Even some cancers can be cured. But doctors actually spend their time treating symptoms and helping patients cope with their medical problems. Physicians also play an increasingly important role in education and prevention. Learning how to motivate people to change their lifestyle is an important aspect of medicine today. You may need to help your patient quit smoking, or eat less red meat and fatty food, or establish a daily exercise program, or administer a shot of insulin. You may spend hours of your day helping a patient cope with her latest diagnosis of breast cancer, or guiding parents through the accidental death of a child, or helping a son cope with the daily problems of caring for a father with Alzheimer's disease. As you can see, the work of a physician uses many skills and covers a broad spectrum of issues.

What Kind of Person Does It Take To Become a Doctor?

What qualities do you absolutely need to be a successful physician in the 1990s? Here is my list of essential attributes:

M stands for motivation.

E stands for effort and education for your entire life.

D stands for desire, dedication, and delayed gratification.

I stands for intelligence, intuitiveness, and improvement.

C stands for caring, compassion, commitment, and communication.

I stands for integrity, inner strength, and inspiration.

N stands for needs (of individuals and society).

E stands for excitement and enthusiasm.

Let's discuss each quality individually.

Without sincere, continuous *motivation*, you cannot become a physician. Motivation is the propellant that is going to get you where you want to go and it must come from within yourself. It will guide you through those tiresome premed science courses and the lengthy and laborious Medical College Aptitude Test. You need it to get through the extremely tedious application process. Once a medical school accepts you, it is essential to keep your motivation high throughout the two years of basic science courses and on through the sleepless nights of on-call duty in clinical rotations, the lack of personal time and time with friends and family, and the seemingly endless years of your residency program. You must realize that you are choosing not only a career but a lifetime commitment of service and education.

This leads us to our second quality. Working together, *effort* and *education* are ongoing for your entire career life. To succeed, diligent effort must go into your premedical education, your extracurricular activities, volunteer work, applications to medical school, your medical school years, preparation for your national licensing examiniations, application for residencies, and your own continuing education throughout your career life. Choosing medicine as a career is choosing a lifetime of effort. You have to exert continual effort to help your patients; maintain your own physical, emotional, and spiritual health; keep your personal life on track; and keep up-to-date in your specialized field as well as medicine in general. Often, sleeping will be a luxury you can't afford. The television will become a foreign object that you vaguely recall as part of your past. Wasn't there a show called "ER" you used to watch faithfully every week? You justified that hour by telling yourself the medical cases were educational! You will never stop studying, reading, and learning. You will feel guilty picking up the latest John Grisham novel when you know you should be reading the medical journal you just received in the mail.

Your education will continue beyond medical school and residency. Once you are in practice, you will have a yearly requirement of continuing medical education (CME) credits. Each state requires a certain number of hours of CME in order to maintain that state's license. The yearly average number of required CME hours is 50. If you attend one professional meeting in Vail, Colorado, for example, and attend 5 hours of lectures and discussions for 4 days, you will earn 20 CME hours for the meeting. All hospitals with residency programs offer frequent noon conferences where you can earn one credit hour of CME. If you are board-certified in a medical specialty, (radiology, for example) you may also be required to earn additional hours of CME credit. Medicine is a rapidly changing field, and all physicians have an obligation to themselves, their patients, and their community to keep up with the changes. Continual reading in medical journals, discussions with colleagues, and recertification exams are all a part of not only your career, but your lifestyle.

Desire, dedication, and *delayed gratification* are our next set of qualities. First, you must have an overwhelming desire to become a doctor; it must be *your own* personal goal. This desire cannot come from your mom or from a wish to follow in a parent's footsteps. You must want to be a doctor because doctoring is what you want to do; because you have a driving need to help people and alleviate pain and suffering, and because you love the thought of the challenge ahead of you.

Along with desire, you also must possess a sense of dedication. A dedication to being the best you can be, to working as hard as you can work, to making personal sacrifices. And a dedication to altruism and selfless giving. This may seem a bit much, but you truly need to possess this kind of spirit or rethink your career goals. One thing this world does not need is more physicians who are only interested in prestige and who view patients only as a dollar sign. Recently I spoke with an acquaintance of mine who also happens to be a physician. During our conversation I asked him about his area of specialty. He replied, "I specialize in neurotic women who have good insurance." Does this sound like a physician dedicated to improving the quality of life? I don't think so. I also know another physician who donates every Monday to a clinic for the homeless. He receives no compensation for his time and actually pays additional malpractice insurance for this privilege. Not only is he a fine example of a dedicated physician, but I am also sure he is more deeply satisfied in his career choice.

The willingness to delay gratification is essential to achieving your goal. It may be very tough for you as you see your friends graduating from college, earning money, taking vacations and buying new cars. Your parents' friends may say, "You mean she's *still* living at home?" Your best friend may be getting married or traveling through Europe for a year, and *you* are frantically studying the gross anatomy of the hand and the biochemistry of amino acids.

If you are contemplating a career change and are currently employed and earning good wages, you will have to make a lifestyle change. No more trips to the Caribbean or a new car every two years. You may need to relocate and sell your house. Putting some areas of your life "on hold" may be something that is extremely difficult for you, but it will have to be done. Medical school is very expensive and it will be a long time before you begin earning a good salary. During your years of residency you will earn a salary, but it won't be large—and you'll have loans to pay back. You'll need to develop a sense of humor about being "a starving student" and a sense of pride in what you are doing. You need to enjoy your unique journey through medical training. Eventually you will finish residency, pay off your loans, make a good income, and have a little more leisure time. But if you are the type of person who is impatient and wants everything *now,* you will become very frustrated and unhappy. You may need to alter your plans and choose a career that can bring you rewards more quickly.

"I" represents *Intelligence, intuitiveness* and *improvement.* Intelligence is defined as a capacity to comprehend facts and propositions and their relations, and to reason about them. It is also a mental acuteness, an inherent, natural understanding. Part of demonstrating basic intelligence is graduating with high grades, earning superior scores on aptitude tests, and problem solving with ease. But intelligence is more than this. It is the ability of quickly relating facts to a result or condition. It is knowing instinctively what to do in a given situation. It is the ability to learn and integrate enormous amounts of material. It is analyzing situations and making quick decisions.

Intuitiveness is closely related to intelligence. It is a quick and ready insight, an immediate cognition. Intuitiveness is difficult to learn, but it is possible to heighten your ability. Reading constantly, listening attentively, using all your senses, being able to observe a situation quickly, and trusting your instincts are all ways to strengthen your intuition.

Improvement is also critical to becoming a physician. You need to evaluate yourself realistically and not be afraid to admit inadequacies and work on improving them. You constantly need to elevate your grades, to improve your communication skills, and to enhance your knowledge of medicine. As you can see, this is a lifetime project.

This leads us to *caring, compassion, commitment*, and *communication*. If one of your goals is to truly satisfy your patients, your genuine concern for them can be just as important as your prescribed medications and treatments. So it is essential that your interpersonal skills support you in showing this concern for your patient's quality of life, feelings, and family. Remember the "old-fashioned," caring doctors who appeared on television? Physicians such as Dr. Kildare, Marcus Welby, and today's Dr. Quinn? In this fast-paced world where time is money, it becomes a challenge to take time and show we care. If you don't enjoy talking and interacting with people and listening to their stories, you cannot show yourself to be a caring, compassionate doctor. Communicating to a patient that his feelings and concerns are of utmost importance to you, with both words and gestures that a patient can understand, is one of the most basic requirements for a future as a physician.

A commitment to your patients, to yourself, and to your community is of tremendous importance to your success. There are times when you will need to make personal sacrifices in order to fulfill your commitment. This will be very challenging, but can also be rewarding. The satisfaction you receive from completing many tasks, from building relationships, from your own sense of value and the sense of value society places upon your skills, should be well worth the commitment.

Integrity and *inner strength* are more important today than ever before. Physicians seem to be targets for censure and criticism. Patients blame their doctors for illnesses that don't respond to medications. Parents file lawsuits against obstetricians for developmental problems in their children fifteen years after birth. Patients sue and lawyers win. Malpractice insurance is skyrocketing. The government wants control, not only over the income you make, but over your treatments, medications, and the tests you order. Frustration becomes a too-familiar feeling. Being a doctor in today's world can be discouraging, when all you want to do is help people feel better. Your inner strength and perseverance is called upon on a daily basis. Your strength of character, honesty, and integrity must be unquestionable, and you must always do what you think is right. If a fellow physician was operating on patients under the influence of drugs, would you allow this to continue? If you observed a cheating incident in medical school, would you report this to a school official? Would *you* cheat if you were in extreme academic difficulty? These are difficult questions and deserve some serious thought. Medical schools can't afford to admit students who are not people of honor. Sure, mistakes are made. We occasionally have incidences where students are dismissed for cheating or acting dishonorably. But this is not the norm. In your application to medical school, you are required to admit to any disciplinary action that has led to any punishment or dismissal in any academic institution you have attended. If you do have any incidences in the past, this may affect your possibility of acceptance. You need to do some serious soul searching and introspection. Are you truly a person with the highest morals and ethical standards? Will you be an ethical physician or one who bends the rules "just a bit" to fit personal needs? Will you help the profession rise to greater heights and build a praiseworthy reputation in the eyes of your community and the country? This sounds a bit melodramatic, but medicine needs young people with honesty, integrity, and the strength to fight for the best care for their patients.

Often you may find it necessary to put the *needs* of individuals and society before yourself. Sleep deprivation, lack of family time, lack of exercise time may become the norm. Patients don't always get sick between nine and five; babies are never born during convenient times; accidents will always occur more frequently after midnight. I also believe that each physician has an obligation to her community. There are countless opportunities to help abused children, battered women, the elderly, and homeless and indigent people who cannot afford medical care. You can donate time to organizations such as the American Heart Association or American Cancer Society or the Boy (Girl) Scouts of America. In the larger world community there are many towns and villages that have rarely seen any health professionals. Some day in the future you will be able, and want, to give back a little of the good fortune you have had.

Without *Enthusiasm* and *excitement* for your career, it will be tough to get through the grind of medical school training. You need to feed your excitement. Get involved in political issues that will affect you as a practicing physician. Volunteer in hospital emergency rooms or free health clinics. Feed the fire of your initial passion for medicine. This enthusiasm will help you reach your goal, not only to become a doctor, but to sustain your career for many years. Your excitement and passion will someday help inspire younger people to pursue medicine.

Are You Right for Medical School?

From the moment you sign your official acceptance into a medical school, you begin a new life! This is a life of constant hard work, of pressure to perform well on exams, of stress from memorizing more and more facts, of living frugally to pay the bills. Stress is a constant. Performance anxiety is high. Belief in yourself and your abilities is constantly tested. Your free time is limited. Exercise is forgotten. Eating a good meal is a thing of the past. Your life is consumed by nerves, organs, tissues, formulas, and diseases. With every disease you study, you begin to have each symptom. A friend asks about your love life. "Love?" you ask, as you look at her in amazement. If you already have a family, you begin to wonder if you'll ever play Monopoly together again. The latest movie? Read a non-medical book? Lay on a beach? Go to a bar? That's history!

Medical school is tough. You will have a new set of problems and new situations to manage. First of all, you will have a heavier workload than you have ever had before. A faculty member once told me, "Medical school, or any graduate education, is like having *two* fulltime jobs." So you need excellent *time management skills*. If you have not utilized time efficiently in the past, now is the time to learn. If you have always depended upon last-minute cramming, you'll have to change that habit. The information overload makes that impossible in medical school. There are volumes of information to master, and this can't be done in two days of non-stop studying. I always compare one week's worth of material in medical school to one quarter of undergraduate education. Memorization skills are important; you may even want to learn mnemonics, a technique to assist the memory. Sometimes there are a few students who drop out before the very first set of exams. These students realize, too late, that this is not the kind of life they want. So be aware that coursework all day and studying for hours at night will be your schedule for the next several years!

Second, you may need to handle *failure* for the first time. At some point in your medical education, you may reach the point of being unable to keep up with the workload. You may be failing gross anatomy or microbiology. You may get frustrated or very discouraged. You may begin to question yourself and your abilities. You may realize that you are unskilled at taking standardized tests. If any of these situations do arise, you must take action. Seek help from your professors, begin counseling, talk to your classmates. Be honest with yourself. I've spent many hours counseling students who are dealing with failure. Some have left medicine, but the majority find greater strength within themselves and turn the situation around. These students go on to highly respected residency programs and become fine, caring physicians. You need to be aware that some type of failure may happen to you, too.

You may find it difficult handling your limited free time. Entering medical school changes your life. Leisure time needs to be scheduled just as your classes are. It is essential to work *free time* into your schedule, but you must realize it will be somewhat restricted. You also need to consider the significant people in your life and work out some time with them. If you have a significant other or are married with children, you can't put their lives on hold just because you're in medical school.

What hobbies do you enjoy? What type of physical exercise do you do? These activities can be added to your schedule, perhaps during a lunch break or when classes are over for the day. You must use your time wisely and include activities that will relax you or help you deal with stress.

Your emotional and spiritual health are also important. Taking time out for yourself, for prayer and meditation, is needed as much as physical exercise. Most medical colleges have religious fellowships. Nurturing your spirituality can provide preciously-needed encouragement and comfort in a very sterile environment.

In many medical schools, the courses may be taught without much integration. You may be expected to *integrate* the various basic science courses on your own. You are not always taught to think or to have opinions. Much of the humanism is taken out of medicine, and you are taught how to treat the disease and not the patient. There may be times when you disagree with your instructor, or feel you are not being treated fairly. You may need to learn to go with the flow rather than try to beat the system. You will need to choose your battles carefully. You can't spend so much time on issues that you compromise your education, yet you also cannot give up your own ideals. You will need to discover the fine line between standing up for yourself and antagonizing the faculty and administration.

There will be some aspects about medical school and clinical work that you love, and others that you hate. Try to accentuate the positive and not dwell on the negative. These four years of medical school will be what *you* make them. You are working toward your goal, learning information and skills that you will use throughout your entire career! Make the most of this wonderful opportunity to learn everything you can. Attend lectures and seminars. Attend your laboratory sessions. Do all the assigned reading and more. It is your responsibility to prepare yourself well for this noble profession.

1

How To Prepare for Medical School

"Believe in yourself! Have faith in your abilities! Without a humble but reasonable confidence in your own powers you cannot be successful or happy."   Norman Vincent Peale

The Written Requirements

Every medical school has a particular set of prerequisites or requirements you must complete prior to entrance. These are usually listed as college courses and/or college degrees. You must check the admissions requirements of every school for which you plan to apply. The Association of American Medical Colleges publishes a book entitled *Medical School Admission Requirements*. This publication lists all the medical schools in the United States, Canada, and Puerto Rico and gives pertinent information about each school. A new addition is published in April of each year. Premedical advisors at every college and university will have a copy, as will admissions departments at all the medical schools. Prerequisites are explained in the sections entitled "Requirements for Entrance."

College Coursework

The majority of medical schools require one year each of biology, general or inorganic chemistry, organic chemistry, physics, and English (usually composition). Many schools require one semester to one year of mathematics. Approximately twenty-three schools also require calculus. Additional

1

requirements may include statistics, behavioral science or psychology, a certain number of humanities courses, and social sciences. A few schools may suggest courses in analytical chemistry, physical chemistry, foreign language, or genetics. If you are planning to apply to one of the schools in Puerto Rico, you must also be fluent in both English and Spanish. Listed below are required subjects and the number of schools which require that subject:*

Required subject	*No. of schools* (n = 117)
Physics	116
General chemistry	113
Organic chemistry	113
English	78
Biology	60
Biology or zoology	55
Calculus	23
Behavioral or social science	17
College mathematics	14
Humanities	11

Most people assume that you must complete a baccalaureate degree prior to entering medical school. In actuality, there are only a handful of schools which state that a Bachelor of Science or Art degree is absolutely required. Most schools declare that the minimum requirement is three years of college or 90 semester hours. On the other hand, most schools which assert that a baccalaureate degree is *not required* also remark that it is *highly recommended*. If you are planning to enter medical school without completing your Bachelor of Science or Bachelor of Arts degree, you must be able to demonstrate exceptional academic ability and have evidence of unusual maturity. By far the majority of students matriculating at a medical school have completed their Bachelor's degrees. The exception to this, of course, are the special programs which combine both college and medical school. Refer to Chapter 5 for more information about these programs. Through my experience with medical students, I have found that students who have not completed at least four years of college have

* Data from the *1993–1994 Medical School Admissions Requirements*, Association of American Medical Colleges.

a slightly increased probability of taking a leave of absence during their first year, or even dropping out of medical school altogether. I feel that those four years are necessary for students to learn about themselves, investigate many career opportunities, and mature enough to make the right decisions for themselves. This is where applicants who have been out of school for a while have an advantage. The older applicant has had an opportunity to be out in the world—with job, work, travel, and life experience. There are also some students who are burned out after four year of college and need a break from studying. There is certainly nothing wrong with taking a year or two off to gain other life experiences.

It is highly possible to prepare yourself for almost any medical school in the United States. To cover all academic bases, I recommend you complete a full year each of biology, general chemistry, organic chemistry, English (primarily composition, but also add a literature course), and mathematics. In your year of math, incorporate a semester of calculus. Adding psychology, another social science, and a few humanities courses is also a good idea. If you have a particular interest in art, theater, music, or a foreign language, include some courses there. And I definitely recommend completing the Bachelor of Arts or Science degree. These four years will be pretty busy, but if you can do well in all the above, you should have an excellent background for medical school.

Should I Take Extra Science Courses?

Often, applicants will be concerned with their science background. There are both pros and cons to adding additional science courses to your schedule. One advantage is that you will improve your general science knowledge. You need your chemistry, biology, and physics background for a foundation upon which to build your basic medical sciences. Also, if your grades in biology and chemistry courses are not as good as you would like, you may want to demonstrate your ability with other difficult sciences. Earning an A in genetics or in vertebrate anatomy can help to illustrate your potential. Biochemistry, histology, embryology, and physiology courses are also traditionally more difficult and can show your science ability. Being able to prove to an admissions committee that you can handle a medical curriculum is of utmost importance.

Second, getting a background in anatomy, physiology, or biochemistry can really help you in your first year of medical school. Most medical students feel that their first year is the most difficult. Coursework is tough, and you need to assimilate volumes of information. Familiarizing yourself with even one of the basic sciences that will be taught in your first year medical curriculum will ease your workload. These courses are often arduous and time-consuming, even at an undergraduate level. You need to do well in these courses if you take them.

Remember, in your first two years of medical school you will be taking a heavy science load. Remember also that your undergraduate years offer you an opportunity that you will not have in medical school. These years are the time to get a broad background in many different areas. It may be the only chance you have to learn about English literature or ancient Egyptian art or the Russian language or modern dance.

One more point: Do not confuse nursing, or other coursework in the general area of medicine, as fulfillment of pre-medical science require-ments. I have had many students, either in nursing or a closely related field, who have wanted to apply to medical school. The courses in such curricula do not have the same content as the more difficult premedical ones. There are no shortcuts or easy pathways. You must take the required courses. Generally speaking, no substituting is possible.

The Unwritten Requirements
People Skills

One of the unwritten requirements of medical schools is having the ability of working well and feeling comfortable with all kinds of people. I can't emphasize this enough! You need to be able to talk with people, listen to them, elicit important information from them, and communicate the feeling that you care about them. There are many different ways you can develop your adeptness with people. Courses on interpersonal relationships and nonverbal communication are available on some college campuses. Mini-courses and seminars on communication are available through churches, schools, organizations, and special interest groups. Psychology and social sciences can help develop your observation skills and understanding of human behavior. Also, take a public speaking course and overcome any difficulty you may have in expressing yourself. The best way to develop people skills, however, is outside the classroom. Work with people. Jobs where you work closely with other people can develop your ability to be a team player. Difficult coworkers or customers provide you with a great challenge. You can use these situations to be intuitive and put yourself in that individual's place. Be charming, thoughtful, and kind and most people will respond positively. Believe me, you will use these skills on a daily basis in your medical work. This is one area where the older applicant with many life experiences has an advantage over a young one just finishing college.

Volunteer work is another way of learning how to deal with people unlike yourself. Choose an ethnic group different from your own, or children, or the elderly with whom to share your time. Learn to communicate with a handicapped, deaf, or otherwise restricted person. The more varied your experiences, the better.

Get out into the real world. Campus life is extraordinarily sheltered. Travel to other parts of the country. Work with the indigent, or inner city youth, or missionaries. Learn about the cost of living, the hardships people have to endure, and the trials people overcome.

Your written communication skills also will have impact in your future career. In your coursework, be sure to include composition and expository writing. You must learn to write legibly. For example, a patient's chart is a legal document, and one which reflects you and your competence. You may be asked to participate in writing journal articles, perhaps a chapter in a book, or writing about your research findings. Throughout your career as a physician, writing skills will be of significant importance.

Extracurricular Activities

Your ability to work with people, your perseverance, your dedication, your competence, and your capacity for hard work will be questioned by admissions personnel. You can demonstrate some of these qualities through the way you spend your free time. Becoming proficient in a musical instrument or a sport is one example. Heading organizations, campus publications, or community projects can help establish your credibility in creativity, reliability, and social concern. Volunteering your services to homeless projects, children's homes, or nursing homes can show your compassion and caring attitudes toward other people. Theater projects can illustrate creativity and originality, as well as improve your ability to express yourself.

Involvement in activities outside of the classroom requires the mastering of time-management skills. You must discover how much time you need for your studies, and then work additional activities into your schedule. You will find it necessary to utilize every minute to its full potential. Spending enough time to do a really good job for a club, fraternity, or other organization, or to become very proficient at a hobby or sport, can be time consuming. But it is important now to learn how best to manage your time, as this will be important throughout medical school, residency, and your years as a practicing physician.

Extracurricular activities can also serve as a stress reliever. Active, competitive sports can burn up stress as well as calories. Music can soothe frayed, pre-exam nerves. Working in volunteer activities can build self-esteem and pride in yourself.

Be Sure To Know What Medicine Is All About!

An important aspect of your preparation for medical school is to learn everything you can about medicine as a profession. It is impossible to know that you want to be a doctor if your don't know what it entails! Here again is where volunteer work or employment comes in. Make time in your schedule to learn about hospital work. Look for job opportunities there, either paid or volunteer. Work in the emergency room. Volunteer to cuddle premature babies. See if you can shadow a physician, nurse, or technologist. Get inside and observe, observe, observe! Talk to employees of the hospital and find out what their jobs are, what they like about hospital work, how they feel about the doctors. Learn about welfare cases, third party payers, Medicare, and HMOs. Make the effort to gain hospital experience, and observe and learn everything you can about hospital life.

Second, find a mentor. Webster's Dictionary defines a mentor as a "trusted counselor or guide." Perhaps you may have a family physician who has been a part of your life since you were born. Talk with her, see if she has any advice for you as a potential medical student. Perhaps you can arrange to shadow her for a few days. Ask lots of questions—discuss primary care and other specialty options. You can't be too informed.

Mentors don't have to be physicians. They can be anyone who can help you and guide you in your plans and decisions—perhaps a counselor at school, a favorite professor, your pastor, or even your high school coach. Search out people you trust, care about, and admire. There are many successful people whose success has stemmed from a mentor. Oftentimes, these people have a desire to repay *their* mentors by helpings others in the same way. A mentor can give you encouragement, discuss personal successes and failures with you, provide insight, and offer suggestions. Sometimes she can give you that extra push that you need to follow through with an idea or plan. You may even find your mentor among your own family.

You also need to read and research. Go to the library and read articles in medical journals. Be particularly aware of the trends in medicine. Learn about malpractice lawsuits, isurance companies, and the latest governmental issues. The Clinton administration has many plans for changing the health care system. Learn how these changes may affect you and your future practice of medicine. Spend some time thinking about emotional medical issues, such as abortion, euthanasia, and AIDS. Develop your own opinions and think about such questions as: "Will I perform abortions?" and "Would I ever assist in a terminally ill patient's suicide?" Your opinions may change over the years, but it is important to begin thinking about these issues now, before you have to deal with the real thing.

Finally, if given the opportunity, get involved in research. Whether or not you want to include research as part of your career, the experience will broaden your horizons. It will help you appreciate the patience, perseverance, and dedication researchers need on a daily basis. Sometimes the smallest step to the answer to a problem will take years of investigation. All medical schools have ongoing research programs and most faculty members are involved in research. Most undergraduate schools have faculty members conducting their own research programs. Learning a current research technique—skills such as electron microscopy, monoclonal antibody production, or gene splicing—will enhance your understanding of basic science. Research is an essential part of medicine. Without it, progress in world health issues, deadly diseases such as AIDS, and new knowledge would be greatly compromised.

2

What Are Medical Schools Looking For?

"Opportunity is missed by most people because it is dressed in overalls and looks like work." Thomas Edison

There are 123 fully accredited medical schools in the United States. Therefore, there are probably over a hundred different ideas about what a school is looking for in a medical student. Each school's admissions administration has devised criteria for their selection of medical school candidates. These requirements fall in three basic areas:

- Academic ability (grade point averages and MCAT scores)
- Extracurricular activities
- Personal qualities

Let's take a look at these three major areas one by one.

Academic Ability

The most obvious criterion for getting into medical school is the applicant's academic record. This record includes the applicant's grade point average, science grade point average, and MCAT scores. Through these numbers, the admissions administrators and admissions committee members can determine whether there is enough evidence of the applicant's ability to accomplish the rigorous academic work necessary to successfully complete the school's curriculum. Simply put, can you do the work? Medical school is not easy. Every year there are students who either drop out or flunk out of medical school and this is not good for either those individual students or the medical school involved. Medical schools hate to see any attrition in their current students. In order to make the best possible choices, we need sufficient information and background on every applicant. We then carefully evaluate factors which may have influenced the applicant's academic performance to date.

Factors Which Influence Grades

There are many factors which directly influence each applicant's grades. Some of these include: 1) the credit hours taken per quarter/semester, 2) the difficulty of the courses, 3) the breadth of education and reputation of the school, 4) life's difficulties and upsets, and 5) whether or not a student has an outside job. This is a lot of information to consider.

The number of credit hours a student takes per quarter/semester is self explanatory. Obviously, a student who takes 18 to 20 credit hours has a much more difficult load than does the person who takes 13 or 14 hours.

The next point involves the rigorousness and difficulty of a student's curriculum. Let's begin with a look at a couple of imaginary students. Susan is a student majoring in biomedical engineering. Every quarter she takes eighteen credit hours or more distributed among several courses in the hard sciences (physics, organic chemistry, molecular biology, biochemistry, zoology, comparative anatomy) along with several courses in either social sciences or humanities. Joe is a student majoring in art history. He takes fourteen to fifteen credit hours per quarter. These hours are primarily distributed among the art and history courses with a few soft science courses (psychology, sociology, philosophy). Joe has a 3.7 GPA. Susan has a 3.2 GPA. Who earns the higher *points* in the minds of an admissions committee member? Probably Susan. Just because a person earns a very high GPA doesn't guarantee him/her instant admission to a medical school. Susan is taking more credit hours per quarter and is taking much more challenging coursework. There are so many other considerations than just the grade point number. We will see more of these factors in the following paragraphs.

Let's gather some more information. Joe attended a small community college for two years, later transferring to a local university for his additional medical school requirements. Susan attended Harvard University in Cambridge, Massachusetts. Who earns the higher credibility? Probably Susan. This is due to the reputation of the school. Characterisitics of a particular college attended are always noted. An especially rigorous program or highly selective college are both important factors which can influence a student's grades. That does *not* mean that an applicant is penalized for where he attends school. A student may not have the means to attend a private institution such as Harvard or Stanford University, but factors such as the school's reputation and difficult coursework are *always* taken into account. In other words, you can earn a form of extra credit by taking on traditionally difficult programs of training or attending recognized difficult schools. You can improve your chances of getting *noticed* by attending an Ivy League school, for example, but to be given proper consideration you must also earn the grades in challenging courses. Whether you attend an Ivy League school or your hometown university, you must earn the best grades possible along with a demanding schedule.

Life will always have its ups and downs. Unexpected problems can wreak havoc with a student's grades. Here is an example: Elizabeth's father was diagnosed with a very serious heart ailment, which disrupted her whole family's life. As a result, her performance in several difficult courses suffered in her sophomore year. Although Elizabeth earned a low GPA that particular year, she did recover and showed steady improvement over the following two years. We always examine these kinds of situations which can affect any student.

The need to work to pay for your undergraduate education is an additional factor we look at. A student who works 20 or 30 hours a week does not have the same amount of time to put into studies as a person who does not need to work. We try to take these situations into account as well.

The overall SGPA (science grade point average) is at least as important as the overall GPA. This number will show an individual's aptitude for science and ability to handle the traditionally tougher courses—chemistry, physics, molecular biology, and genetics. Joe, for example, has earned an overall GPA of 3.7. His grades have been all As. However, in most of his science courses Joe has had difficulty earning any grade higher than C. This fact will not bode well with the admissions committee. The members will doubt his scholastic ability when faced with the rigorous basic sciences coursework of medical school.

Additional Factors

Additional factors that admissions committee members look at are:

Trends. We look for trends in an applicant's academic performance. For example, that D+ in general chemistry that David earned during his freshman year may not be held against him if *all* his other science grades are good and have improved. The difficult time Elizabeth had during the year of her dad's illness also affected her performance. Since she was later able to pull her grades up, this upward trend will definitely be taken into account. The fact that a student shows an upward progression in her GPA helps demonstrate her drive and perseverance, as well as her determination to overcome problems and obstacles that are a part of life.

Well-rounded education. Not only do medical schools want the students to have excellent GPAs and SGPAs, they also want to see that the applicant is *liberally* educated. They want to see a balanced education, with courses evenly distributed amongst the natural sciences, social sciences, and humanities. If Susan had only taken engineering and science courses, she would be somewhat one-dimensional. Well-rounded education is very important to admission committee members. Languages, music, art, and history are just as important as all those sciences.

Disadvantaged background. The social and cultural backgrounds of applicants are considered as well. The fact that a student comes from a very disadvantaged background will influence the committee. Different cultures and economic conditions can influence how a student performs in an academic setting. Lack of sufficient finances creates the need to work, which in turn will no doubt affect a student's GPA. Perhaps Joe comes from a family who cannot support his education financially. He needs to work 25 to 30 hours per week as a waiter to pay tuition. The committee will most certainly take that into account when examining his academic record. A student who must spend so much time in a working situation rather than studying his organic chemistry will probably not earn the A he wanted.

MCAT Scores

As far as the results of the MCAT goes, a student needs to do as well as possible. She needs to take time to prepare for the exam. The results of this exam are another tool that admissions committee members can use to evaluate a potential candidate's scholastic ability and aptitude for the medical profession. Each medical school has a *number* that is needed for actual progression through the application process. This number, of course, will differ from school to school. There are schools that will not look at an applicant who does not have double-digit MCAT scores. These are scores which are 10 or above in each subject area. Other schools may consider aplicants with lower scores who have shown academic excellence in other areas such as science courses, work in research, or graduate degrees.

The main point of all this information is that each applicant *must prove scholastic ability*. The committee must hear "Yes, I can do this work!" loud and clear. Medical schools do not like to take risks. If a school accepts an applicant, the school wants to be as sure as possible that the applicant will progress, without academic problems, through the four year curriculum. You must prove to the admissions committee members that you have the academic aptitude to do the work. This is the bottom line. You can demonstrate this through your GPA, your SGPA, or your MCAT scores. If all three areas are at the breaking point, you'll need to find a way to improve at least one, and preferably all, of these major areas.

Extracurricular Activities

A second important factor concerning an applicant's application is the extracurricular activity section. Included in this area is work experience. How a student spent summer vacations is also considered. An individual's capabilities, initiative, and creativity cannot always be measured by traditional systems of grading. How an applicant chooses to spend time outside of the classroom can help give an admissions committee member insight into that student. Some of the qualities that medical schools are looking for include:

Knowledge of, and exposure to, needs of individuals and society, awareness of health-care delivery systems, evidence of leadership, and knowledge of the demands and rewards of a career in medicine. Evidence of personal growth, humanitarian concerns, life experiences, community involvement, and achievement in an area outside of academia are also pertinent to the committee.

How can you possibly demonstrate all this? You cannot. But, you can look through this list, perhaps think of qualities you have, and concentrate on one or two areas. Think about the activities with which you have been involved. Think about how each of these activities has helped develop leadership, communication, or creative skills. Let's take an example. Sherry has always loved competitive sports. She is particularly skillful at track and field events. She has spent much of her free time training for meets and competitions. This demonstrates great perseverance and dedication on her part. She has also developed physical skill and stamina over the years. This stamina and perseverance will help see her through the rigors of medical classes and long grueling hours on call at the hospital. In addition, Sherry volunteered two nights a week at a clinic for the homeless. Sherry is clearly interested in service to the community and society. Medical schools are getting more and more involved with service to their own community, and faculty are impressed when they see young people who are sincerely dedicated to helping others. This is clearly a very important aspect of being a dedicated physician.

How about another example? Ken has played piano since he was five years old. He has dedicated an enormous amount of time to his music. He improvises for hours and he plays in a trio on weekends to earn extra money for tuition. He teaches youngsters how to play. Ken's special hobby illustrates his manual dexterity, his devotion to learning something new, and perseverance.

Admissions committee members love to see that an individual has a life outside of school and classes. They want to know that the student can bring something unique and special to their school and to medicine. Not everyone can have a special talent. But it is important to see yourself as unique. You need to do some heavy thinking. What do I like to do? How do I spend my free time? Do I have any special aptitudes? What do these activities illustrate about me? What makes ME me?

Personal Qualities and Attributes

Perhaps the most subjective area in judging an applicant's potential is the area of personal qualities. Although critically important, personal attributes are difficult to determine through your application and interview. Some of the qualities that medical admissions people are looking for in their potential students include:

intelligence, problem-solving skills, critical judgment, originality, creativitiy, integrity, empathy, warmth, caring, emotional stability, kindness, compassion, motivation for medicine, reliability, honesty, social concern, stamina, good language skills, dedication, perseverance, the ability to make positive contributions to society....

The list can go on and on. You need to learn to assess yourself. Where are your strengths and weaknesses?

Think about your life from the time you first began school. What subjects interested you most? Were you always the leader? Were you the bookworm? Social butterfly? Class clown? What do you truly enjoy doing? In what extracurricular activities have you participated? What do these activities show about you? Are you the confidante of your entire dorm? Do you enjoy teaching? What forces drive you to pursue a career in medicine?

Imagine interviewing these two candidates for medical school admissions. One is bubbly, warm, enthusiastic, and has highly developed interpersonal skills. The other applicant has a very formal manner, never smiles, and exudes no interest in spending the hour with you. Which doctor would *you* like to see come through the door into *your* hospital room?

Personal qualities can be difficult to determine and are very subjective. These qualities need to be developed over your lifetime through your experiences and influenced by your family and friends. Why don't you ask a friend or relative what they think are your best qualities? You may be surprised at their answer. A friend of mine (who also happens to be a psychiatrist and *very* insightful) once told me that she thought I was very creative. "Creative?" I replied in shock. "Me?!" I've always remembered that statement, and it became important to me. Ever since then I have seen that I *am* creative and I have worked on developing that part of me.

Additional Items of Importance

There are other parts of an individual's application that are also of extreme importance and not to be taken lightly. These include:

The Personal Statement,
Letters of Recommendation,
and the Interview

The first two items are covered in Chapter 3, "Understanding the Application Process." The personal statement will give the committee some insight into you as a person. It should show your interests, accomplishments, and your motivation for medicine. This will tie into the personal qualities and attributes that the members of the committee are trying to determine about you. Your letters of recommendation should give the committee insight into your past performance, motivation, work ethic, and those very essential personal attributes.

The interview will also be dealt with in depth in Chapter 8. This process will be critical to your successful selection. There is only one medical school I know of which sends a specially devised evaluation form to each student in lieu of an interview.

Residency Status

Finally, you must take into consideration your place of residence. The majority of schools are state schools and are funded by the state. These schools are going to offer seats in the first year class primarily to in-state students. A few schools do not offer any seats to out-of-state students. You will automatically have your best chance of acceptance at schools in your own state. The east and west coast state schools are notoriously difficult for applicant acceptance. Students must be superior in every area. Schools in the midwestern parts of the country tend to be slightly easier for applicant acceptance into their programs. However, those schools will still give preference to their own residents. If you're not an Ohio Buckeye, it will be tougher to get into Ohio State. You need to check out the percentages of out-of-state students each school accepts. Check with your pre-med advisor, call the medical schools of interest to you, or call or write to the Association of American Medical Colleges. People at the AAMC headquarters in Washington, D.C. compile that data (and more) about each accredited U.S. medical school.

Who Is the "Perfect" Medical School Applicant?

So who is the "perfect" medical school applicant? Medical schools are looking for diversity in their classes. They want people from all backgrounds, races, and ethnic groups. There are students who range from 20 to 45 years of age. Of course, the perfect applicant would have; 1) a 4.0 GPA, 2) 15s on his MCAT, 3) worked as a research assistant and orderly at an inner-city hospital, 4) volunteered at a children's camp for the disabled, 5) spent a couple of years travelling throughout third-world countries teaching the natives sanitary techniques and simple health techniques, 6) phenomenal interpersonal skills, 7) talent in music, art, and sports. Does this person exist? We would love to find medical students of this caliber, but we are dealing with real people, with both talents and faults.

Just for fun, let's come up with a profile of a "perfect" applicant. This person's name is Chris. We will not determine if Chris is male or female or a minority candidate. This does not have any significance at this point. However, for the sake of reading ease, I will use the feminine pronoun.

Chris grew up in a very small town in the Midwest. Ever since she could remember, medicine was fascinating. Chris owned many pets, constantly hovering over the birth and death of cats, dogs, birds, and rabbits. Chris joined the biology club in high school, later becoming president. She sought out her family physician as a mentor. This physician had become a friend through Chris' problems with asthma as a young child. Chris' many trips to the emergency room became fun as she joked with the nurses and watched other patients being treated. Chris began her studies at a good state institution, where she majored in biology. Chris minored in Spanish, as she loved foreign languages. Chris felt she wanted and needed a well-rounded education in the humanities as well as a good science education. Chris loved dabbling in oils and watercolors. She also began learning about art history and perfecting some of the techniques she had learned during extra classes taken at her local art museum. Chris began to develop additional skills. She started to use her Spanish when she volunteered at a free clinic geared to the indigent migrant workers every summer. Chris worked diligently and learned to have deep compassion and empathy for the hardworking migrants. During Chris' second summer, she was offered a paid position as a receptionist in a dental practice. Wishing to learn more about actual hospital work, Chris talked to her old family physician, who then helped arrange a job for her as a nurse's assistant in the community hospital's emergency department. These two time-consuming jobs were difficult to juggle along with her intense course load. However, Chris maintained a 3.7 GPA. Chris' SGPA was even more impressive—a 4.0. Chris began to realize that she was becoming quite stressed due to her time commitments with her work schedule, school, and sorority. She decided it was time to begin a regular exercise program. Running four miles a day before classes took discipline, but Chris was determined and persevered. While tutoring younger students in chemistry and physics, Chris learned patience and diligence. She decided to take the MCAT in the fall of her senior year. She had just completed all her chemistry, biology, and physics courses. Chris registered to take the MCAT, confident of her ability. Chris received an 11 in the physical sciences, a 13 in the biological sciences, a 12 in verbal reasoning, and a Q in the writing sample. She was on top of the world!

And then disaster struck. She was informed by her father that he and her mother were getting a divorce. Chris felt her perfect family was falling apart. Beginning to have some doubts about everything, Chris still completed the Bachelor's degree with honors. Chris decided to wait to apply to medical school until she had seen some of the world. For six months Chris travelled across the country, stopping to see friends, working occasionally bussing tables. Chris finally ended up in the hills of West Virginia at a place called the Red Bird Mission. Chris spent a year there utilizing past skills learned as a nurse's assistant, working in the medical clinic. Chris helped teach good health habits to kindergarteners in the small country school. She also helped build a new addition onto the small medical clinic.

The more time Chris spent in the clinic, the more her old desire to become a doctor arose. So Chris decided to head back home and begin the tedious application process. Hoping that her three years spent working, volunteering, and travelling would not affect her chances adversely at acceptance, Chris stressed the importance of those life experiences. Chris also decided to take a few graduate courses to help demonstrate her continued academic ability. She took both biochemistry and vertebrate anatomy and earned As in both courses. Chris also went back to her old job as an assistant to work in a hospital setting until August, when she hoped she would matriculate.

How would you rate this applicant? Do you see evidence of scholastic ability? Has the applicant participated in extracurricular activities, hobbies? How does she handle stress? What are some of her strengths and weaknesses? Is there evidence of personal growth and maturity? Has she been involved in community service? Is there evidence of personal qualities such as integrity, compassion, sensitivity toward others, and desire to work and help people? As you can see, the answers can be derived from careful examination of the student's profile, the work she's chosen to do, the experiences she has had, and the broadness of her education. Of course, there is always some subjectivity involved. Even when a factor looks black and white, some committee member will fing shades of gray. For example, I personally look at Chris' three years post-college as a plus. Having life experiences, meeting many people, seeing the real world, working and taking responsibility for herself shows initiative and guts. Chris matured a great deal during those three years and widened her horizons, she can bring what she's learned to her medical school years and her practice of medicine.

Medical schools and their admissions committees evaluate every single applicant with utmost care. The tools they utilize are only tools. There is the human factor involved as well. No two committee members will view one single applicant in the same way. There are many variables. The most important thing that you can do is to:

- Learn about yourself.

- Look at your application from an objective point of view.

- Try to determine how to best sell yourself.

3

Understanding the Application Process

"The impossible is the untried."   *Jim Goodwin*

As you begin preparing for the long and tedious application process, it is easy to feel overwhelmed. What is all this stuff? The application looks very intimidating. And what do all these words and initials mean? Let's start out by giving you some basic information concerning the whole process.

General Application Information

The Association of American Medical Colleges (AAMC) is a nonprofit national organization whose main purpose is the advancement of medical education and the nation's health. The society comprises 126 accredited U.S. medical schools, 16 accredited Canadian medical schools, approximately 400 teaching hospitals, along with 90 academic societies and faculty, medical students, and residents. The Association is interested in strengthening the quality of medical education at all levels. The AAMC is responsible for the Medical College Admission Test (MCAT) and the American Medical College Application Service (AMCAS).

AMCAS is a centralized application processing service for applicants applying to 110 participating U.S. medical schools. It was developed by admissions officers of schools belonging to AAMC. The purpose was to

19

facilitate the process of applying to U.S. medical schools. As you can imagine, the thought of filling out separate application forms to 10, 15, or even 30 medical schools would be overwhelming!

All people who are applying to AMCAS-participating schools must submit application materials to these medical schools through AMCAS. The AMCAS process benefits both the participating school and the applicant by coordinating all application data and saving both school and applicant time and expense during the application procedure. So, simply put, you pick up one application, fill it out, send it to AMCAS, and they take care of the rest.

Only those 16 schools which do not participate in AMCAS (such as Harvard Medical School, Columbia University School of Physicians and Surgeons, Brown University School of Medicine, Baylor College of Medicine, and Yale University School of Medicine, to name five) have their own applications. You can obtain those applications directly through that school's admissions office. When you've completed the application, you send it directly to that school.

Where and When to Apply

First of all, keep this rule in mind: *The earlier the better*. Get all your materials together in a timely fashion. Be organized. This whole procedure is time-consuming and often tedious, but your future is dependent on your results.

Second, never miss a deadline. Use the Personal Admissions Planner in the back of this book to keep track of your applications and deadlines.

Where you apply is up to you. But here are a few factors you might need to consider:

State of residence. Many state schools accept the majority of their students from applicants who live in the state. Often, tuition is extremely high for an out-of-state student. For example, at the University of Colorado School of Medicine, the tuition for a resident of Colorado for the 1995–96 school year is $9,565. For an out-of-state student, the tuition is $41,618. That is a lot of money and a significant difference. If I were from Illinois, for example, I doubt very much if I would apply to that school. The out-of-state tuition is prohibitive. Most schools have considerably lower fees for the residents of their state. These schools know that many students remain in the state where they attended medical school following graduation. The state is spending a great deal of money to educate medical students, so they would much rather keep them in their home state!

Private vs. state. State-supported schools are required to give preference to state residents. Some private schools may receive financial support from their state goverments, also. However, there are many private schools who accept far more non-residents than residents. In most private schools, tuition is the same (high) for both in-state and out-of-state students. Tuition is always higher at private institutions. Most fees range from $20,000 to $30,000 per year.

WICHE and WAMI. No, this is not a foreign chant or religious hymn. WICHE stands for Western Interstate Commission for Higher Education Professional Student Exchange Program. WAMI refers to Washington, Alaska, Montana, Idaho. These programs are regional agreements specifically to aid states which do not have a medical school. In the WICHE program, all accredited western medical schools, except University of Washington, will accept students from Alaska, Montana, and Wyoming as in-state students. The accepted students from these states will not be required to pay out-of-state tuition. This is a program that seeks to remove penalties to students from states without a medical school.

WAMI is a program organized through the University of Washington School of Medicine. Students in the states of Washington, Alaska, Montana, and Idaho may take their first year of medical training at participating universities in their home state. The students transfer to University of Washington in the second year, finishing up with clerkships at participating hospitals for their third and fourth years. This program was begun as a means to distribute physicians throughout the states, in both rural and urban areas.

Combined degrees. You may wish to attend a medical school which has combined degree programs, such as B.S./M.D. programs, M.D./Ph.D. programs, M.D./J.D., or M.D./MPH programs. See Chapter 5 for more information about these combined degree programs.

All medical schools listed in the various AAMC guidelines and publications are accredited by the Liaison Committee on Medical Education. These schools maintain high standards and seek highly qualified applicants. Medical schools do differ, however, in several ways. They vary considerably in student body size, size of the faculty, type of patients in the associated hospitals, personality of the current students, general philosophy of education, student services, sources of financial support, types of financial aid available, and opportunities in special areas such as research. You need to consider all these areas and look into each and every school carefully. You will be spending four years, and possibly residency training time, in that location, with those faculty, students, and administrators. You need to choose a school where you will feel comfortable and happy.

Application Fees

Application fees vary from school to school. The fees can range from $10 to a high of $95 (at Boston University). If you consider the average fee to be $35, and you apply to fifteen schools, you'll be spending $525 just in application fees! That does not include the AMCAS service fee, which is based on the number of AMCAS-participating schools to which you are applying. Application fees can really add up, and unless you are independently wealthy you may need to pick and choose carefully. Don't forget you'll also incur traveling expenses for interviews.

The Application Itself
General Suggestions

The very first thing you need to do is to request transcripts from *each* college you have attended. This means every one, whether or not you earned any credits from that institution. Perhaps you enrolled in a school for a summer but did not finish the course or it was non-credit. AMCAS still wants to know this, even if it seems silly to you. Include junior colleges, trade schools, graduate schools, or professional schools within the United States, Canada, or U.S. territories. One set of *official* transcripts needs to be sent by the registrar directly to AMCAS. At the same time, you should ask for your own personal copy. It will be very useful when you are filling out your AMCAS application.

AMCAS begins accepting transcripts on March 15. It is always a good idea to keep in mind that the earlier, the better. Don't wait until the last minute. Don't wait for final quarter or semester grades. You can have those sent later.

Deadlines

The date that AMCAS begins accepting applications is June 15. Do not send any materials, other than transcripts, before this date. They will be returned to you. In the case of the sixteen schools which do not participate in AMCAS, please check with the individual school for the date of the earliest receipt of applications. They all vary. Check the deadline dates, as well. This date is just as important, or more! The deadlines for the AMCAS-participating schools vary also. Deadlines range from October 15 to December 15 for most U.S. AMCAS schools.

Filling Out the Application

The application itself is pretty much self-explanatory. The most important rule is: *Be honest*. Answer every question on the AMCAS application with truth. AMCAS will be checking all information carefully. So don't falsify anything, for not only will you embarrass yourself, but you may permanently affect your chances of ever being accepted to a medical school.

A second rule is: *Be neat*. Don't handwrite your application. Type it or have someone type it for you. First impressions are very important here. No one wants to spend the extra time deciphering illegible handwriting or sloppy typos.

Third, make a photocopy of everything. You will need to look over your application periodically. You may fill out your application in June and not have an interview until January. Reread your application before every interview to refresh your memory on what you wrote in your personal statement, your best courses and grades, and other points you might have stressed in the application. You may think, "How could I forget?" But you can.

The Importance of the Personal Statement

The Admission Committee members and Dean of Admissions will note your coursework and grades. They will read your MCAT scores. They'll look over your extracurricular activities, hobbies, jobs, and volunteer work. But before the interview, these people have no idea who YOU are. Within the application is a blank page for you to fill in. The personal statement is a means of letting the readers take a real look at you. It is a glimpse into your life and experiences and what motivated you to choose medicine as a career. It is a great opportunity for you to talk about yourself in a different way, separate from grades, school, and numbers. It will demonstrate your communication skills. I can't tell you what to write, you need to work on that on your own, but I can give you some hints on what not to do!

Do not leave the space blank. The committee members will assume you either had nothing to say or couldn't be bothered. There is no excuse not to use this page to your advantage.

Do not use the space to merely reiterate what is on the application. The reader has already noted such areas as your courses, grades, and test scores. Rather, use the space for explanations, for stressing your strong points, for discussing what led you to medicine, or for talking about turning points in your life or special events that may have changed you. Talk about skills you have mastered and what you've learned from your experiences. Discuss your creativity or your imagination, your leadership or teamwork skills, your determination and perseverance.

Do not waste this opportunity to prove to the admission committee that you are different from the norm. Show them that you need to be seen and heard to be appreciated. I can't tell you how often I have been about to reject a candidate for an inteview, but after spending a few extra moments reading the personal statement I changed my mind! Treat this page of your application with the greatest respect.

Write several draft copies of the personal statement. Give them to people whose opinion you truly respect (friends, relatives, professors, or counselors) and who you know will read it objectively. Listen to their suggestions, particularly concerning the English language, not necessarily the content. Be sure you are expressing yourself clearly. Be especially neat when typing the statement onto the specific page of the application. Again, neatness and readability are significant.

Don't use the passive voice in your writing. If you do not know what this is, look it up or see an English professor!

Letters of Recommendation

Get to know the people who are your professors, mentors, employers, and supervisors. It is crucial that the people who will be asked to write a letter of recommendation for you know you both personally and professionally. Don't ask a professor to write something as important as a letter of recommendation to medical school unless she is familiar with your academic potential, your work habits, your motivation, and your ethics. If you have never had personal contact with a professor except to sit through his lectures with 150 other freshmen, this is not a good person to ask to write a letter. It doesn't matter if you earned the highest grade of the decade on her final exam. If she only knows this one fact about you, that's all she can say. I personally have read many reference letters for applicants which have said, "I don't really know this student...." I then wonder about this applicant's judgment. Is this the best person the applicant could come up with? I can't say this enough: You must get to know your professors and mentors and let them get to know you. No one can write a good letter of recommendation if they don't know the student they are writing about. These letters can be critical to your acceptance. Do not minimize their importance.

Supplemental Applications

Before I discuss the supplemental application, I want to explain "Three Steps to Accepts." There are actually three steps in the decision-making process. When you complete your application for AMCAS, you list the schools to which you want to apply. The first step in gaining entrance to a medical school happens when these schools receive your application. The first decision made by the school, usually by the dean of admission, is "Do I want any additional information on this student?" If the answer is no, the applicant will receive a "thanks, but no thanks" letter. More often than not, unless the applicant shows extremely low scores and numbers, the answer will be affirmative. The applicant will then be asked to fill out a supplemental application and to have letters of recommendation sent out. The majority of schools have their own personal supplemental application. This application is usually short, with a few additional personal questions. Many schools request a picture along with the supplemental application. The picture is most useful in recognizing the candidate when re-reviewing the application. Hundreds of applicants come in for interviews, and while it is hard for us to remember names, we rarely forget faces. It is very helpful, so please comply with this request.

The second step is to determine the interview status of an applicant. This decision may be made by the committee, but if the school receives many thousands of applications, the decision may be made by the dean, associate dean, or assistant dean. If the decision of whether or not to interview is fluctuating, the final decision will usually favor the applicant. It is always better to err on that side, as it can't hurt the school to interview a few extra candidates.

The ultimate, or final, decision is made at the admission committee meetings. This is where the voting takes place. A candidate will either be accepted, rejected, or put on a waiting list. Chapter 6 has more information about the admissions committee.

The Medical College Admissions Test

"Failing to plan is planning to fail."   *Ben Franklin*

What Is It?

The Association of American Medical Colleges (AAMC) developed the Medical College Admissions Test (MCAT). This exam was created by medical school administrators and officers, pre-med instructors, medical educators, practicing physicians, and a group of testing experts. The main purpose of using the scores of this examination is to help admissions committees predict which applicants will successfully complete the medical curriculum. The MCAT provides admissions committees with a standardized measure of academic performance for all examinees under equivalent conditions. In other words, the exam results provide a way for admissions committees to compare the qualifications of applicants from a variety of undergraduate schools. The extent to which test results are used in the admissions decision varies from one medical school to another. For more information on this, see Chapter 6.

In 1991, the AAMC introduced a substantially different test. This test was designed to encourage students interested in medicine to pursue a broad undergraduate study in natural and social sciences along with humanities. The MCAT assesses each applicant's mastery of basic science concepts in biology, chemistry (both general and organic), and physics. The exam also tests scientific problem-solving ability, critical thinking, and writing skills.

When To Take It

The MCAT is given in April and August/September of each year at specific, established centers. These centers are located primarily at colleges and universities. There are 372 testing centers located across 50 states, with an additional 35 centers located in Guam, Puerto Rico, Virgin Islands, and Canada. The recommendation of most medical school officers is that you take the MCAT in April of the year prior to the September in which you plan to apply to med school. For example, if you are planning to begin medical school in the fall of 1997, you would register to take the MCAT in April, 1995. If you are in undergraduate school, this time falls in the spring of your junior year. At this time you will have completed one year of biology, one year of general chemistry, one year of organic chemistry, and one year of physics. I recommend the April testing date for two reasons: 1) You will probably receive your results of the exam in June. Therefore, medical schools will receive the scores just as applications begin arriving. 2) If you do not do as well on the exam as you had hoped, you can plan to retake the exam in September. You can organize a new game plan for study, and the September MCAT results will arrive at medical colleges close to, or soon after, the application deadline. Usually if a candidate's application is going before the admissions committee, the chairman of the committee or dean of admissions will hold off the vote until the scores have been received.

The Format
Registration

You *must* register to take the exam. Registration materials are available through undergraduate premedical advisors and medical schools. You will need to pick up the current year's *Announcement: Medical College Admission Test*. This is a booklet which describes the examination and gives you registration dates and deadlines. Inside, it has an envelope which contains registration materials. You need to complete and mail the following materials: the Candidate Information Folder, the signed Identification Card with a current passport-type picture of yourself attached, and the appropriate registration fee. These materials must be received by the MCAT Program Office by the appropriate deadline. This deadline is approximately two months prior to the exam date. If you are late in getting together your registration materials, you may register through late registration procedures. You will need to enclose all materials noted above plus a nonrefundable late fee, which is usually about $50. The registration fee for 1994 was $150. This may change slightly from year to year. My advice is to always plan ahead. Ignorance is never an excuse. It is your responsibility to organize yourself and your time and to be aware of all deadlines. The price for not doing so may be $50 or may put your medical education off for another year. There are also additional fees required if you wish to take the exam on a Sunday or to change your testing center, for example. If you have a disability, you may need to request special arrangements. Along with your registration materials, you will need to send a letter describing in detail the special arrangements needed, and a letter from your physician or other certified specialist that gives a professional diagnosis of your disability and your need for these special arrangements.

The Day of the Exam

Try to relax. Have a good breakfast. Set your alarm clock with plenty of time to spare. You will want to arrive at the testing center relaxed and ready. You must report to the test center no later than 8:00 A.M. Prior to the examination date, usually about three weeks after your registration is received, a test center admission ticket will be sent to you. This ticket shows the exact address of the test center, the time at which to report, and the date for which the ticket is valid. If you need special accommodations, this will be indicated. Be sure to check all of this information for accuracy as soon as you receive it. You must bring this ticket with you to the test center, and you will not be admitted without it. You will also need to bring official personal identification. This identification must have a photograph, such as a driver's license or student identification card. The photo which you sent with your registration materials will have been sent to the testing center and the two photos will be examined and compared. Only people who are positively identified will be admitted. You will also be asked to sign the back of the MCAT identification card to certify its authenticity and to confirm your intention to apply to a health professions school. Your thumbprint will also be taken and placed on your card. Remember to bring three soft-lead (no. 2) pencils, an eraser, two ballpoint pens with black ink for the writing sample, and a watch to help you keep track of the time. All this security can be a bit formidable, but get used to it. You'll encounter similar procedures, if not more stringent, when you are taking your medical licensing examinations.

Once you are admitted, the supervisor will assign you a seat. You will not be allowed to eat, drink, or smoke in the testing room. All instructions will be given to you by the supervisor. You will have two ten-minute breaks and a sixty-minute lunch break during the day. The test supervisor will report any examinee who violates any of the test regulations or exhibits irregular behavior. So be cool. Be honest. This is *not* the time to be questioning authority.

The Examination

There are three sections, each consisting of a total of 219 multiple-choice questions. There is a section on verbal reasoning, physical sciences, and biological sciences. The verbal reasoning section assesses your ability to understand, evaluate, and apply information presented to you in passages of approximately 500 words. These passages include areas of humanities, social sciences, and natural sciences. The physical sciences section is designed to assess your knowledge and reasoning in general chemistry and physics. The biological sciences section examines your reasoning skills and knowledge of biology and organic chemistry. Both sections will consist of general questions and problems. The writing sample consists of two essays. You will have two 30-minute sessions. Each writing sample will provide a specific topic which requires an informative and descriptive response. You will not be scored on knowledge of the subject matter, but on your skills in developing a central idea, synthesizing ideas, presenting these ideas in a logical manner, and writing clearly, utilizing proper grammar, punctuation, and syntax.

How To Prepare for the Exam

Preparation for the exam begins with your undergraduate courses. You'll need to have general chemistry, organic chemistry, biology, and physics under your belt. These courses should provide the basic skills you'll need for the two science sections. You should also add various humanities, social sciences, and writing composition to your undergraduate training. Once you have completed these courses, you should test your knowledge. Send for the *MCAT Student Manual* from the Association of American Medical Colleges. This manual provides you with sample questions, explanations to those questions, and responses. Included is a sample MCAT exam. You should set up a time to take this practice exam. This will enable you to note your deficiencies and go back and study these subject areas.

There are also books written on the MCAT Examination. These books include hundreds of sample questions and timed tests. These are available through campus bookstores, as well as local bookstores. Examples of these are the Barron's Educational Series and Petersen's *Guide to the MCAT*. Practicing the art of taking timed, standardized exams and answering lots of questions will give you experience and knowledge of what is involved in the actual MCAT.

Some candidates enroll in commercial review courses to help them perpare for the examination. These programs are usually fairly costly. The benefit in these courses lies in the fact that if you have spent money on the course, it will force you to spend time reviewing and taking the tests. You can achieve a sense of accomplishment and preparation and improve your self-confidence. These tests and programs can help to demonstrate your weak areas. You can then go back to your course notes and textbooks and review them. These review courses will not help you, however, if you do not put a certain amount of time into it. If you do, the course can help you with motivation and organization. You cannot decide to prepare for the MCAT in just two weeks. If you find it difficult to motivate yourself in organizing your time and going back to review your organic chemistry or physics on your own, signing up (and paying for) a review course may help give you the motivation you need.

Preparation for the MCAT is the key. The exam scores can be a deciding factor in whether or not you are ultimately accepted by a medical school. The exam should not be taken lightly. You should begin your review about five to six months prior to the date of the exam.

Your Scores

Four individual scores, one for each section, will be sent to you and the medical schools you have designated on your form. These scores range from a low of one to a high of fifteen for the verbal reasoning, physical science, and biological science section. The writing sample is scored differently. You will receive two scores per topic. These scores are on a scale of 1 to 6. These numbers will then be converted to an alphabetical scale ranging from J (the lowest) to T (the highest). Along with your scores, you will also receive information to help you interpret where you stand with other examinees. You will receive information concerning the ranges of percentile ranks, score means and standard deviations, and percentages of examinees who received each scaled score. With your permission, MCAT scores will automatically be included with your AMCAS application materials, and will be sent to any AMCAS school to which you apply. If you have taken the MCAT serveral times, your two most recent scores will be reported as part of the admissions information.

What do your scores mean? Seeing all these numbers can be very confusing. The first item to consider is where you stand among other students who took the MCAT. You will find this as you read through the information sent to you with your scores. Check the percentile ranks. This will give you an idea of where you rank in comparison with all others who took the exam on that particular date. The percentiles change slightly each time the exam is given. For example, in September 1992, receiving the score of 10 in biological sciences would put you in the percentile range of 80 to 90. If you earned the score of 6, you would rank in the 20 to 32 percentile range. Each medical school puts varying weight upon the results of the MCAT. Some schools will not interview applicants who do not score 10 or above in each category. Other schools will take other factors into consideration, and applicants with fairly low MCAT scores can still be offered a chance to interview with the possibility of acceptance into their medical program. Usually the applicants in this category are people who may have been out of school for a number of years but have exceptional grades and other achievements.

The AAMC Section for Student Services sends out to each medical school an Admission Action Summary. This summary has an enormous amount of data concerning all applicants to medical schools for a particular year. Included in this summary are average MCAT scores. The chart below shows the average 1993 MCAT scores of all applicants and the average scores of all accepted applicants broken down into categories:

Total Applicants		*Accepted Applicants*	
VERBAL REASONING	8.3	VERBAL REASONING	9.6
PHYSICAL SCIENCES	8.2	PHYSICAL SCIENCES	9.7
WRITING SAMPLE	0	WRITING SAMPLE	P
BIOLOGICAL SCIENCES	8.3	BIOLOGICAL SCIENCES	9.4

Men (Accepted)

VERBAL REASONING	9.6
PHYSICAL SCIENCES	10.1
WRITING SAMPLE	P
BIOLOGICAL SCIENCES	9.9

Women (Accepted)

VERBAL REASONING	9.6
PHYSICAL SCIENCES	9.0
WRITING SAMPLE	P
BIOLOGICAL SCIENCES	9.4

Minorities (Accepted)

VERBAL REASONING	8.1
PHYSICAL SCIENCES	7.6
WRITING SAMPLE	N
BIOLOGICAL SCIENCES	8.0

If you do not perform well on the exam, should you take it again? This is a question many applicants ask themselves. If you were ill, did not prepare, or did not take some of the coursework you should have had prior to the exam, by all means take it again. If you do repeat the exam, make some changes. Prepare. Study hard. Take several practice exams. Sign up for a commercial review course if you can afford it and you truly think the course will help you. Do not sign up for the exam and take it just to see if you increase your score. *Both* scores will show up on your application. Admissions committee members will carefully look at how much you improve your score. If you do not think a second exam will improve your scores, then it is probably wasting your time and money. Seek some advice from premedical counselors or admissions officers at a medical school. Ask them how your scores compare with the average matriculant at their school. This may help in your decision.

5

Alternatives to the Standard Application Process

"Convert problems into opportunities."   *Dennis Waitley*

Early Decision Program (EDP)

It is of utmost importance to get your application in as early as possible. That is why it is also important to take the MCAT in the spring of the year in which you are sending in your application. Another way to assure that you receive early consideration is to apply to the Early Decision Program, or EDP.

In this program, you chose *one* school to which you apply. This can be your first choice or the school where you feel you have the best chance of being accepted. All the other admission steps are the same, except you must submit this application to the medical school by their deadline.

In 1993 there were 88 medical schools which participated in the EDP. Check the AAMC's *Medical School Admission Requirements* to see if the school you are interested in has this program. You can also call the medical school to find out the answer.

Each EDP applicant files one application through AAMC. Your application must be received at your school by a specific date, usually some time between mid-June and mid-August. The admissions committee meets and makes their decisions. EDP applicants are informed of their acceptance or rejection by October 1.

In 1993, there were 2,934 EDP candidates. Of these, 1,165 (or 39.7 percent) were accepted. If you are rejected, you are free to begin the application process to other schools. If you are well qualified and have a preference for a particular school, the Early Decision Program may be a good one in which to participate.

The main advantage of this program is that you have an answer by October 1. If you are accepted, you can relax and forget about other applications, traveling for interviews, and worrying!

Early Admission

There are a few medical schools which have an early admission program. This is *not* to be confused with the Early Decision Program. This is a program in which a medical school has set up an agreement with a local undergraduate institution. Undergraduates who have chosen medicine as their career choice and have completed their first two years of undergraduate coursework with exceptional grades are eligible to apply. A committee with representatives from both institutions selects a small number of students. These students are officially accepted to medical school.

The advantages are: the student is not required to take the MCAT exam, the student can relax and not go through the trials of the regular application process, and the student has the choice of beginning medical school following the junior year. This also saves the student money, as the fee for the MCAT currently runs at $150, and application fees can add up to thousands of dollars. There are conditions, however. The accepted student must continue to perform well in courses, as the medical school has the final say prior to that student's matriculation. Of course, the student must also complete all academic requirements for that medical school.

Flexible Curriculum Program

Many schools are now offering flexible curriculum agenda for a selected number of minority or disadvantaged students. The flexible curriculum is designed for students who may encounter academic difficulty during the basic science years, usually years 1 and 2. These programs offer the medical curriculum over a 5-year time frame, rather than over 4 years. You need to contact the individual school to find out whether or not they offer such a program.

B.A. or B.S.–M.D. Degree Programs

These are also referred to as combined college/M.D. programs. There are currently 30 such programs across the United States. Admission to these programs is open to a select number of very highly qualified high school students who have chosen medicine as their career goal. These programs usually take from 6 to 8 years to complete. During these years, the student earns both his undergraduate B.A. or B.S. degree along with his medical degree.

Most schools with this program generally require courses in biology, chemistry, physics, English, and social studies. State-supported schools most often only accept their state residents. Private medical schools don't ordinarily limit themselves to state residents.

Besides excellent academic credentials, medical schools look for exceptional maturity, leadership skills, high motivation, and extracurricular activities. Frequently the programs also require specific scores on either the ACT or SAT.

Medical Scientist Training Program

There is a definite need for physicians who are able to conduct medical research and interpret scientific data. In order to train students in both the areas of basic sciences and clinical sciences, the National Institute of General Medical Sciences began a combined M.D.–Ph.D. program. This program is called the Medical Science Training Program, or MSTP.

Medical scientists differ from basic scientists because they have medical training. They also differ from physicians in that they have extensive research experience and training. In 1993–94, the federal government supported 822 MSTP students.

The MSTP grants are made to universities and their medical schools. Generally, there are about 150 positions available each year. Thirty-two schools currently offer the Medical Scientist Training Program. Applicants must have U.S. citizenship and be highly motivated individuals with exceptional research and academic potential. MSTP provides financial support for their students in the form of both paid tuition and a yearly stipend. Students' performances are evaluated periodically for renewal of the grant. It usually takes approximately 6 years to complete the program.

M.D.–Ph.D. Programs

In 1993–94, 115 schools offered a program designed to give students the opportunity to earn both the Ph.D. and the M.D. degree. The Ph.D. is earned in an area related to medicine, such as pharmacology, immunology, neuroscience, or cell and molecular biology. These programs differ from the MSTP in that the students are not funded through the federal government. Occasionally there is institutional money to help students in this program. Another source of financial aid could exist through an individual faculty member and his grant support.

M.D.–J.D. Programs

There are currently six medical schools where a student can participate in a program designed to earn a law degree along with the M.D. These schools are: Chicago–Pritzker, Duke, University of Illinois at Urbana–Champaign, Southern Illinois, University of Pennsylvania, and Yale.

M.D.–MPH

One school offers a combined medical degree with a Master's degree in Public Health, designed to be completed within four years. This program is available at Tufts University School of Medicine in Boston. This is a challenging program for a very select number of students. Students should have a definite interest in examining the changes in population composition, the structure of health care delivery, and environmental, economic, and social factors which shape health care services delivery.

Final Notes

If you are interested in any of these kinds of degree programs, you should get in touch with the medical schools in which you are interested. The school can then send the information directly to you. You can also seek the advice of counselors, either at the high school or college level.

6

The Medical School Admissions Committee

"Always bear in mind that your own resolution to succeed is more important than any other one thing."   Abraham Lincoln

When you hear the words "medical school admissions committee" do you break into a cold sweat? Does your heart begin to pound and your stomach do whirlies? If you answered yes, you are not alone. Most applicants feel confused and helpless when they think of the mysterious admissions committee. What do they do in those two-hour meetings? Are they totally destroying the credentials of an unknown victim? Do they tear down each personal statement and reference letter, laughing hysterically over the audacity of the people that are applying with *those* MCAT scores?

Most likely none of these things is happening in the notorious meetings behind closed doors. The committee members themselves are merely faculty members you see every day. Let's take a little mystery away from this group and show you what goes on.

What Is the Purpose of the Committee?

The Medical School Admissions Committee is a group of faculty members who have the responsibility of selecting the following year's first-year class. The medical school, as well as the faculty, consider this to be one of the most important committees in the institution. Basically, the future of the school depends in large part on this committee and its decisions.

Along with selecting the school's future students, the committee is responsible for any new policies that go into effect concerning admissions procedures. They also keep up with the latest trends in medical school applicants. For example, if the members know that there will be an all-time high number of applicants that year, they may change some of the recognized standards and be more selective. Back in the late 1980s, the number of applicants dropped considerably. The necessary grade point average and MCAT scores were lowered slightly to accommodate and fill the medical school classes. The trend of the last few years is directly opposite, because the interest in attending medical school is rapidly rising and there are more applicants from which to choose. Other policies may include such issues as handicapped applicants. Each medical school must develop and publish their own technical standards for the admission of handicapped students in accordance with legal requirements.

Interviewing prospective candidates is a big part of the committee's work. At some schools, interviews take place with all the members of the committee at the same time. Usually in this case the number of committee members is small. At other schools, all of the faculty members at the institution are asked to participate in the interview process. In this case, candidates will usually interview with two members of the faculty, usually one clinical and one basic science professor. One, both, or none may be members of the admissions committee. However, each interviewer fills out some type of form which discusses his or her reactions and knowledge of the applicant.

Each member of the committee is expected to have reviewed the entire application packet for every applicant. These materials include the application itself, all academic reports and MCAT scores, personal statement, reference letters, and interview reports. Every member then evaluates the candidate, notes both strong and weak points, and discusses the qualifications with the rest of the group.

Who Are the Committee Members?

There are two types of faculty members at a medical school. The first professors you usually encounter are those who teach one of the basic science courses. These basic sciences include anatomy, physiology, biochemistry, pathology, pharmacology, and microbiology and are taught in the first two years. The majority of these professors have a Ph.D., or doctorate, in that particular science. Some, however, may have an M.D. or possibly both degrees. A second type of faculty member is a clinical professor, who teaches in a clinical area such as surgery or pediatrics. These faculty members are M.D.s and teach in the third and fourth clinical years.

The admissions committee is composed of both basic science and clinical science professors. Usually the committee is about half and half, as both types can bring their unique perspective to the proceedings. There can be as few as five or six, or as many as fifteen or sixteen. The number varies from school to school.

Most committees also have one or two student members, usually in their second year. Either the dean of admissions or the committee chooses the student members. Students apply for a position on the committee and it is considered an honor to be chosen. It also happens to be many extra hours of hard work and quite a responsibility, so the student really has to want to put this time into admissions.

Some schools also have one or two members-at-large. These are physicians who are working in the community and have an interest in the future doctors of America.

Most medical schools have a rotating membership on their admissions committee. Each faculty member serves a term of approximately two or three years. Usually about a third of the committee rotates off, while a new third comes on board. This way there are always seasoned members to help the new members learn the ropes.

What Do the Committee Members Look For?

Each and every committee member brings his or her own personal ideas and standards to the meetings. One member may be a real stickler for MCAT scores. Another may feel grade-point averages are much more reflective of a student's capabilities. Others may feel communication skills or research experience is mandatory. So it is difficult to generalize about the committees. You may want to reread Chapter 2 and review what medical schools are looking for in potential students. But I consider the following five points to be the prime issues.

Can the student make it through? This is the bottom line. Does the student demonstrate with coursework, test scores, and aptitudes that she can persevere and perform well in both basic science and clinical work? A great amount of time, effort, and finances is put into each student who accepts and begins medical school. If the student consistently fails courses and needs extra years to complete training, more and more money and resources are being used. Most schools are on tight budgets and can't afford to do this on a continuing basis. They want to train the student and graduate her on a timely basis.

Does the student show sufficient motivation for a career in medicine? It is very important that a person knows what he is getting into with a career in medicine. The most successful applicant has demonstrated eagerness in learning about the medical field. He has sought out mentors and hospital experiences. He has spent time with volunteer projects and honed skills in observation and communication.

Is the applicant committed to many years of difficult schooling and training? Ability to commit to long-term goals is essential to surviving in medical school. Usually this trait is obvious through facts in the application. If a student has successfully committed herself to other programs or projects and has demonstrated how she has reached other goals, that is a good sign that she will fulfill the promise of becoming a physician.

Will the applicant make a caring physician? Both the interview reports and certain parts of the application should give some clues as to the empathetic and sensitive nature of the applicant. Letters of reference will often remark as to the presence or lack of such qualities. Interviewers are often trained to be aware of any red flags in this area, such as obvious aloofness or prejudices.

Does the applicant show sincere interest in the school? The interview should reveal whether or not a student is interested in attending the school. There are some students who have no intention of accepting an offer at a particular school, but use the interview as a practice session.

This usually comes through in the interview. It is a waste of our time to send this person a letter of acceptance. However, if you show great enthusiasm for a particular school, praise the program and the people you have met in a genuine fashion, this can go a long way with an interviewer. It is only natural that people like you when you like them.

How Are Decisions Made?

Do you remember the "Three Steps to Accepts" explained in Chapter 3? Let's review them:

1. The actual application is reviewed. A decision is made to either reject the candidate at this point or to ask for the applicant's supplemental application and letters of recommendation.

2. The application, including the letters of recommendation and supplemental application, are reviewed. A decision is made whether or not to interview the applicant.

3. Following the interview, the candidate is evaluated carefully by the admissions committee.

So here we are with the admissions committee. Members of the admissions committee meet on a regular basis. In the summer, the committee discusses plans for the upcoming year, makes changes in their policies, works on interviewing techniques, and tries to improve on what they accomplished the previous year. Applicants for the early admission program are interviewed and discussed. At the start of the fall session. or quarter, the committee is in full swing. In order to give full attention to all applicants, the committee often meets every two weeks. As the year progresses, and if there is an exceptionally large number of candidates, the committee may assemble every week.

The members make the ultimate decisions at these committee meetings and this is where the voting takes place. As the applicant's name comes up, that person is considered for a place in the first-year class. Each member of the committee may bring up different aspects of the application, interview report, general impressions, or reference letters. Discussion is very valuable and the interviewer will usually be present to offer impressions. Each committee member's questions may be answered by the interviewer or other members of the committee. Finally, a vote is taken. The student can be 1) offered acceptance, 2) rejected, or 3) put on a waiting list.

People are human. Members of the admissions committee are human. Therefore, there will always be a certain amount of subjectiveness in the decision-making process. But you must trust that these people will make the best decisions possible.

You will then be notified of the commitee's decision. Some schools send out acceptance letters on a weekly basis, as the committee meets and makes their decisions. Other schools send out all their acceptance letters on a specific date. Don't be afraid to ask about each school's policies. You don't want to be biting your nails for three or four months anticipating an answer, if letters aren't sent out until March!

7

Success for Non-traditional Candidates

"Don't wait for your ship to come in; swim out to it."   Anonymous

The total U.S. population has changed in the last decade. Minorities have grown—currently representing almost one in five Americans. Nevertheless, minorities in medicine are still underrepresented. Medical schools are committed to increasing the numbers of minorities in medical care, teaching, and research. In 1969, the Association of American Medical Colleges (AAMC) developed the Section for Minority Affairs. Then in December of 1988, this section was incorporated into what is called the Division of Minority Health, Education, and Prevention. The Division has two major missions: 1) minority medical student preparation and the medical education pipeline; and, 2) disease prevention in medical education and health programs.

First, let's define who is a minority and then discuss the minority medical school issues.

Who Is a Minority Candidate?

The underrepresented minorities include: African–Americans, American Indian/Alaskan Americans, Mexican–Americans, and mainland Puerto

Ricans. The focus is on increasing the number of successful applicants from these four groups of people.

The problem is not in the lack of interest in health fields, for minority students do show a definite interest in the health professions. A survey in the *American Medical News* (January 4, 1993) found that more than 5 percent of African–American college freshmen are interested in medicine, compared with 3 percent of white students. Somewhere along the line, minority students are lost in the crowd. Some may lose interest, of course, but others may be pressured by financial concerns and lack of familial and other support.

Why are minority applicants being denied admission?

Most medical school administrators agree that the main reason minority applicants are not accepted is the fact that inequalities exist in early educational opportunities. This lack of early learning skills and opportunities then leads to poorer high school grades, college grade point averages, and MCAT results. In particular, MCAT scores are a problem. This is due, most likely, to two reasons. First, most minority students actually earn lower MCAT scores. Second, there is an overreliance on standardized test scores. These two problems, then, limit the chances of otherwise successful candidates. Perhaps too much importance is put on test results. Who knows what factors are present during that one day of testing?

Most faculty members are willing to help increase minority representation in their schools. However, college grades as well as MCAT scores have been lower for minority students than for white students. College grades are often dictated by standardized testing and it is a fact that most standardized tests are geared to middle-class America. No wonder underrepresented minorities are "disadvantaged." So in the numbers game, minority students often lose. And the main problem is that faculty members balk at lowering their academic standards. Therefore, we need to get away from the school of thought that a standardized test score is the major indicator of intelligence or a predictor of success.

Another factor which influences minority students is financial aid. More minority students come from low-income families than do white students. The prospect of coming out of medical school with huge debts is rather discouraging.

Additionally, many minority candidates are woefully ignorant about the application process. They don't play the game well. Some minority students are even discouraged by their premed advisor.

But, take heart. Both the AAMC and many medical schools, themselves, are actively seeking change.

What Is the AAMC Doing To Help Increase Minority Participation?

The AAMC has established several programs. These include:

- Project 3000 by 2000

- Medical Minority Applicant Registry (Med-MAR)

- Publications

- Help in the financial aid arena with fee waivers and special financial aid programs through National Medical Fellowships, Inc.

Let me tell you a little about these programs.

Project 3000 by 2000 began in November of 1991. Its purpose is to eliminate the underrepresentation of African–Americans, American Indians, Mexican–Americans, and mainland Puerto Ricans in U.S. medical schools. The goal is to increase the number of these minorities entering medical school each year to 3000 by the year 2000. The AAMC believes that academic medical centers have both the means and the responsibility to improve educational opportunities for minority young people in their communities. Also, they conclude that medical schools have not and will not be able to solve the problem alone. They must work in partnership with high schools and colleges. Project 3000 by 2000 is creating a network of community partnerships composed of school systems with a high enrollment of minorities, colleges that are interested in increasing *their* graduates entering the health field, and academic medical centers that are also committed to increasing the opportunities for minority students. Programs in the schools should begin no later than the ninth grade.

This is a big task. But the program is making progress in accomplishing these objectives. The number of minorities in medical school declined in the 1980s. But minority representation in the fall of 1993s freshman class set a record—minorities made up 11.2 percent of total admissions.

Back in 1969, two medical schools, Howard (in Washington D.C.) and Meharry (in Nashville, Tennessee) accounted for 75 percent of all minority students. But by 1979, these two schools accounted for only 20 percent. Minorities are accepted in all U.S. medical schools today. And they will continue to increase until, in the year 2000, there will be 3000 or more minority students working on their Doctor of Medicine degree.

The Medical Student Minority Applicant Registry (Med-MAR) is a service initiated by AAMC for minority students. All minority students can participate in Med-MAR by indentifying themselves as belonging to an underrepresented minority group or as individuals from a low-income family. Each individual fills out a questionnaire when taking the MCAT examination. Two Med-MAR lists are published annually (for the two MCAT sessions) and these publications are then distributed to all U.S. medical schools. This program enables minority or otherwise underprivileged applicants to have their basic information circulated throughout the country automatically. The registry contains the following information for each student: name, address, state of legal residence, date of birth, social security number, undergraduate college, and MCAT scores.

This is a great service for minority and disadvantaged applicants. It puts information at the fingertips of all medical school admissions personnel. I highly recommend that each minority candidate or underprivileged applicant participate in this service.

Publications. I have just told you about the Med-MAR publication. Another publication that is available through AAMC is called *Minority Student Opportunities in United States Medical Schools*. This provides students, premedical advisors, counselors, and other interested people with up-to-date information and descriptions of programs at medical schools. These specified programs are designed to provide opportunities for underrepresented racial and ethnic groups to pursue medical careers.

The information gathered for this publication was through both the medical schools and the AAMC Student and Applicant Information Service. The book contains entries from medical schools with descriptions which cover seven topics:

1. Recruitment

2. Admissions

3. Academic support programs

4. Summer and enrichment programs

5. Student financial assistance

6. Educational partnerships

7. Any other pertinent information

This book is very useful, as it provides you with information as to the number of underrepresented minority applicants, the number who are offered acceptance, the number who matriculate, the number enrolled in the entire school, and the number of graduates. Besides statistical data from 127 medical schools (Puerto Rican schools are included), specific programs are described. Some schools have partnerships with undergraduate colleges. Some have summer programs that are targeted for undergraduates who plan to apply for medical school. Other schools have great support programs primarily concerned with academics of enhancing skills in test taking, time management, note taking, study habits, and preparing for licensing examinations. All this information is worth taking a look at.

Besides academics, schools may have special student organizations such as the Student National Medical Association, whose members participate in educating local junior high and high school students. Additionally, each individual school may have financial aid available specifically for underprivileged and minority medical students.

These publications should be used in conjunction with *Medical School Admissions Requirements* for the year you intend to apply for admittance. For additional information concerning these materials, you should get in touch with either your premed advisor, an admissions dean of a medical school, or the AAMC:

> Association of American Medical Colleges
> 2450 N Street, NW
> Washington, D.C. 20037-1126
> (202) 828-0400

Financial aid. National Medical Fellowships, Inc., or NMF, is the only national, private, not-for-profit organization that provides financial assistance to minority medical students. The minority groups it serves are African–American, Native–American, Mexican–American, and mainland Puerto Ricans. Since the founding of this organization, it has extended nearly 22,000 awards which total over $32 million.

The skyrocketing costs of medical education create a definite barrier which affects the ability of potentially successful minorities to pursue a medical career. African–Americans, Mexican–Americans, and Native–Americans are more likely to come from lower income families. Loans are available, but the thought of being over $100,000 in debt is overwhelming to a young student who has little familial support. Many minority students come from families unable to provide even a portion of the funds needed to complete medical training.

Contributions to National Medical Fellowships, Inc. come from corporations, foundations, private individuals, and former NMF scholars. This organization offers awards to students enrolled in the first or second year of medical school, based on financial need. If you are interested in more information, or an application, write or call:

> National Medical Fellowship, Inc.
> 254 W. 31st Street, 7th floor
> New York, NY 10001
> (212) 714-1007

The Dean of Minority Affairs, or the Dean of Student Affairs in any medical school will also have this information for you.

What Are Medical Schools Doing To Help Minority Applicants and Matriculants?

As mentioned previously, medical schools are trying to gain the interest of minority applicants. Schools are actively recruiting minorities, with the help of Med-MAR. Admissions committee members are being educated about the problems facing minority candidates. There is also an underrepresentation of minorities on the faculty and administrative staffs of most medical schools.

Each medical school has its own private sources available for financial aid to minority students. This money is usually provided by endowments and grants made to the school. A list of contact people for each institution is listed in several publications of the AAMC, including *Medical School Admission Requirements* and *Minority Student Opportunities in United States Medical Schools*. Additionally, many schools will waiver their application fees for disadvantaged and minority applicants.

Medical schools are establishing many academic support programs and summer enrichment programs. Academic programs include peer–tutorial programs for students having academic difficulty and student mentor programs to provide social, emotional, and academic support through an upperclassman. There are other helpful activities such as faculty advisor programs, national board preparation courses, academic support seminars, and various counseling services.

Many medical schools offer great summer programs. Some of these include specific programs to help students in the application process. There are special workshops on interviewing strategies, test-taking strategies, time-management skills, and programs designed to improve students' performance on the MCAT. Other schools offer summer research apprenticeship programs where students highly motivated for a health-career take classes and work with a faculty mentor in the laboratory. Other programs for high school students focus on strengthening academic skills and motivation.

Most schools also offer a 6 to 12 week prematriculation program designed for incoming first-year students. Lectures and labs are provided, as well as instruction in study skills, time management, and stress mangement.

Descriptions of programs at each U.S. medical school are available in the publication *Minority Student Opportunities in United States Medical Schools*. You should make every effort to contact the medical schools in your area and find out what programs are offered.

Are Women as a Group Considered a Minority?

In 1969, only 9.4 percent of first-year medical students were women. In 1990, the percentage increased to 40.2 percent, Many medical schools across the country have now reached or exceeded the 50 percent mark in the number of women medical students. By 1990, the United States had more than six times as many women doctors as it did in 1963—up to 104,200 from 17,300. Times have certainly changed. Women have more opportunities in the 1990s than they have ever had.

So, to answer the question, No. Women are no longer considered a minority in medical schools. Back in the seventies and early eighties, women did have a slight advantage. Medical schools were actively seeking to admit women medical students. The belief that women encounter prejudice in the application process to medical school is no longer valid. The acceptance rates for men and women in 1993/94 were virtually the same, 40.5 percent and 40.6 percent respectively.

Support for Women

Women medical students have different needs than their male counterparts. Often, women have less confidence in their academic abilities. They feel more stress and pressure at exam time. If women students are in a relationship, married, or have children, they are often the keeper, or nurturer, of the relationship. They are still the primary caregivers of their children. Although men are changing, they may not be as in touch with the needs of children and spouse. So, study times may be more limited when a woman has responsibilities other than medical school.

All these factors affect the stress level and academic performance of women students. They often need emotional support. Many medical schools have a dean for women who is a specific contact person for women's needs and problems. Another source of support is an organization called the American Medical Women's Association. Most medical schools have a student chapter of this organization. AMWA members often provide housing for women interviewees during the admissions process. The group also provides female physician mentors, seminars and lectures by women physicians, and support groups for women.

How Has the Increase in the Number of Women Physicians Changed Medicine?

Just two decades ago, women still felt that the only way they could be successful physicians was to eliminate the idea of marriage and family. Women almost went to the other extreme to prove that they were no different than their male colleagues. I was guilty of this back in the early 1980s. I was the sole female faculty member in a department of anatomy, and I hid my pregnancy from my male colleagues until the day I went into labor! (Although I must admit I did go into labor three months early.) I didn't want to see the change in attitude of my fellow professors who would no longer feel I was serious about my career or would assume I couldn't uphold my share of the departmental responsibilities.

Female physicians, in general, make an effort to balance their medical practice with family. Most are not willing to sacrifice everything for their career. In fact, they are often willing to sacrifice some career advancement in the short term. It has always been easy for male physicians to have families, mainly because their wives took care of home and children. Today, there is more sharing of all responsibilities. Many male physicians are putting more emphasis on family time.

Men, as well as women, are questioning the 60 to 90 hour work schedule that has, too often, been the norm for any physician. Job sharing and part-time residency programs will become more available in the next 10 to 20 years.

The Older Applicant

I personally love to see older people in the applicant pool. The older applicant has several advantages over a student fresh out of undergraduate school. These include: life experiences; maturity; knowing who you are and what you want; and possibly money saved. (I am certainly *not* saying that a younger applicant cannot possess these particular qualities.)

According to statistics, the older applicant does have a lower chance of being accepted to a medical school. The percent of students accepted appears to be inversely proportional to age. Here are the 1993–94 numbers, taken from the *1995–1996 Medical School Admissions Requirements*:

Age	*Percent accepted*
20 and over	69.9
21–23	46.2
24–27	33.4
28–31	30.7
32–34	30.9
35–37	28.1
38 and over	21.9

This decrease in the percentage of acceptance could be due to many factors. Some students have not fulfilled all requirements. Some do not have the background of the younger applicants. And often MCAT scores are lower because older applicants have been out of school for a number of years and don't have the test-taking skills that are needed.

What Does the Older Applicant Need to Do?

As an older applicant, you need to review your record thoroughly, preferably with the help of a premed advisor. Obtain your own copy of your transcripts. Make an appointment with a premed advisor or with an admissions administrator at a nearby medical school. Determine if you are lacking any undergraduate courses. If you are, plan a schedule for completing those courses. Work hard and obtain excellent grades.

Take an MCAT preparatory course. You need to bone up on test-taking skills and the information which will be covered in the exam.

Reflect carefully on your life's experiences. Be able to show the number of skills you have learned. Be able to write and talk about what you have learned through your previous schooling, jobs, volunteer work, travels, etc. Relate what you have learned to a career as a physician.

Carefully decide who you can ask to write a good reference letter. Be sure to include at least one person who knows your *academic* ability. Be sure the others can address your aptitude for medicine.

The most important thing to remember is this: Use your age to your advantage!

What About the 22-Year-Old White Male?

There have been many occasions when I have talked with medical school applicants and the first thing I am asked is, "I'm a white male. How can I ever get into medical school?" Well, the competition is pretty stiff. But it is stiff for all applicants. As we saw earlier, the percentage of men who were accepted for the 1993–94 school year was virtually the same as for women. The difference was only .1 percent.

Everyone gets into medical school on their own merit. Sure, occasionally a student slides in because of personal influences—a parent is a faculty member or a grandparent was the dean of medicine. But this is not the norm. It is up to you as an individual to prepare well, focus on your goals, and make proper use of all opportunities available to you.

8

Interviewing

"When in doubt, tell the truth."   Mark Twain

Every medical school receives thousands of applications per year. Each application is thoroughly reviewed at least twice prior to the selection of candidates for the interview. The total number of applications is eventually cut down to approximately 10 to 20 percent of the original number; these applicants are then offered the opportunity to interview. For example, if the school receives 5,000 applications, only 400 to 600 applicants will be offered a chance to interview. Very few schools do not require an interview. The only one of which I am aware is the University of Iowa College of Medicine. Their admissions committee uses a specially devised evaluation form to evaluate the personal qualities and characteristics of the applicants in whom the school is interested. This form is sent to selected people and used in lieu of a personal interview.

Very few medical schools have funds available for interview trips. Occasionally, one medical school will use the interview reports from another medical school if requested by the student. This usually happens only under extenuating circumstances, such as extreme financial difficulty or the fact that the applicant is out of the country. For example, several years ago a young woman applicant requested that our admissions committee evaluate her without the benefit of an interview. She was willing to accept our decision based on her written application, academic record, letters of reference, and her personal statement. Not participating in the interview, an integral part of the application process, actually puts the medical school applicant at a distinct disadvantage. This young woman, however, was out of the country working with the Peace Corps. She had an excellent record, superb letters of recommendation, a beautifully written personal statement, and was doing admirable work with people of another culture. She *was* accepted; but this situation is, by far, the exception to the rule. Most applicants utilize the opportunity of an interview to their best advantage.

A few schools across the country offer regional interviews, usually as a service to help cut down travel costs for applicants. These interviews are conducted at selected locations throughout the country. Loma Linda School of Medicine, George Washington School of Medicine, the Uniformed Services University of the Health Sciences, F. Edward Herbert School of Medicine, and Harvard School of Medicine are a few schools which offer this service. Additionally, at the request of applicants, the University of Medicine and Dentistry, New Jersey School of Medicine will allow an applicant to be interviewed by an alumnus of that school. These options are the exception, however. The majority of medical schools conduct their interviews on their campus, utilizing their faculty, administration, community physicians, and students to do the interviewing.

One other point is important. *Never call a medical school and request an interview.* This is not your decision to make. This is a decision that belongs exclusively to the admissions administrators and/or committee members. There have been times when aggressive students have called me and almost demanded an interview. I usually make note (not a positive one!) of that fact in the candidate's admissions file. Not matter how strongly you feel that you will make a terrific doctor, to ask for an interview is totally inappropriate. You may call the admissions office to inquire if a decision to interview you has been made *if* more than a few months have passed since your application was mailed. But do not extol your virtues over the phone and tell us that we are idiots if we do not choose to offer you an interview.

How Important Is the Interview?

The interview process is one of the most important steps in your quest to gain acceptance into a medical school. No matter how good your numbers (GPA, MCAT) are, most medical schools are interested in who you are as a person. The purpose of the interview is twofold.

The admissions committee members want to know about you as human being. Are you warm and likeable? Can the interviewer visualize you as a colleague? Are you going into medicine for the right reasons? What makes you tick? What do you get excited about? Do you have a realistic idea about medicine? Are you friendly and compassionate? How do you handle yourself in the interview? Are you answering questions easily and honestly? Medical school faculty need a personal interview, not just application papers, to answer those questions. Remember, the interview is a means of personalizing the application process.

The interview day gives you an opportunity to visit the medical school campus. You can see the location of the school, ask questions about the school, meet students, faculty, and administrators. It is very important for you to get a feel for the school. Do students seem happy? Do the students speak highly of their professors? Do you like the city and state where the school is located? Is the campus safe? Are the students proud of their school? Is there adequate classroom space? How about the laboratories? Do you like the library? Is the school computerized? Are people friendly—not just the students, but the secretarial staff, security officers, librarians, custodians? The general pervading atmosphere is very important and you should get a sense of this by the time you leave the campus. It is also important for you to feel welcome and special. You are a potential student. Do the school, students, and faculty help you feel wanted or are they intimidating, treating you as a number?

It is important to realize that the interview is not just a formality. The interview may make you or break you. But also recognize that *you* are interviewing the school as well. You, too, are trying to make a decision. You are checking out the students, faculty, and facilities of the school. Reminding yourself of this fact may help you relax during your interview day.

How To Prepare for the Interview
Research

The first step you should take in preparing for your interview is to thoroughly *research yourself*. Think about your life. Of what are you most proud? What goals have you set for yourself in the past few years? Have you accomplished those goals, and if so, how? What qualities do you possess that will help you become an excellent physician? How did you come to this decision? Has there been one special person in your life who has been a mentor to you? What distinguishes you from the 5,000 applicants who have applied to this particular school? What experiences have you had that have helped you become a better person? What activities, classes, or work do you enjoy most? What do you most delight in talking about? These are just a few sample questions that you should spend some time contemplating.

Another suggestion is to *journal*. Spend an hour each night on a topic you would like to discuss with an interviewer. Write about it. Put down everything that comes to your mind. Think about what led you to your career decision, about significant events in your current life or childhood, and about people who have made a difference in your life. If you faithfully do this for a week, month, or even a year, you will find this material very interesting to read at a later date. You may learn something new about yourself. This exercise will also help you put your thoughts in order. You will have some control over what you talk about in your interview. Be sure to have some topics ready that you can speak about fluently and articulately.

The next step is to *learn about each school* which has offered you an interview. You absolutely must have a minimum working knowledge about the school. You do not have to memorize the number of students who have graduated from the institution, or when the school was founded, or how many students have chosen pediatrics as their specialty. But check out some general information. How large is the school? How many people apply each year and how many students are in the first year class? Is the school located near shopping? Metroparks? Other universities? If you are interested in research, are there funds, facilities, and opportunities for students? Is the campus located in a metropolitan area? Carefully look over any brochures or catalogues you have obtained from the medical school. Find the positives and negatives about the school. Write down everything that you would like to know and don't find in the brochure. You may think you will remember these questions, but when your anxiety level begins to rise on your interview day, they will fly out of your memory banks. So be sure to write them down.

Practice

This may sound silly, but practice talking about some of the ideas you have established about yourself or qualities you would like to demonstrate to your interviewer. Find a roommate, sibling, parent, or better yet, a premed student or medical student who has been through the interview process.

Prepare a list of questions that may be asked in your interview. Have one of these people ask you questions as if you were actually doing the real interview. Do this several times. It is amazing how fluent you become when you actually begin to organize your thoughts. Practice will not make you perfect, but you will gather insights about how you think on your feet. You will be more nervous, anxious, and trying harder to please during your actual interview. However, the more you talk, answer questions, and journal about yourself, the better you begin to know yourself, your motivation, and your skills.

Prepare Ahead

Hopefully you are reading this chapter many months before you expect to hear about your interviews. If not, these few words of advice are probably too late for you. Take a good look at yourself. Is your weight appropriate for your height? Have you been to the dentist and had your teeth cleaned and checked? Do you smoke? Now is the time to make a checklist. Begin to work on the areas of your health that need improvement. Medicine today is very preventive oriented and physicians are expected to be role models in society. A person wishing to become a physician needs to be aware of this very important trend. If you smoke, you are going against preventative medicine. Most Americans are aware that smoking is a leading cause of many cancers as well as heart disease. Weight, recreational drug and alcohol use, and lack of exercise are some areas of your life that may need assessment. You need to do these evaluations before the admissions committee does!

There is one other thing that is very important for you to do. *Know what is happening in the field of medicine.* Medicine is rapidly changing. The future of health care is uncertain. It is very important that you know about medical/legal issues, malpracice, and government regulations and controls. You need to familiarize yourself with recent legislation that is currently under review or being proposed. Know about President and Hillary Clinton's health plans and how they will affect both you as a practicing physician and the general population of this country.

You also must understand the significance of HMOs (health maintenance organizations) and PPOs (preferred provider organizations) and third-party payers. You must research areas unfamiliar to you. Spend time in the library, talk with practicing physicians, read newspapers and medical journals such as the *Journal of the American Medical Association*. Be knowledgeable and informed.

Keep up with newsworthy events. Don't be afraid to share your opinions. During the most recent Presidential election, I often asked my interviewees how they felt about the candidates. "What do you feel are our country's major health-care problems?" I would ask. "Who do you feel has the best solutions?" I was amazed at how few of the applicants knew what was going on in our country. A very meager number appreciated the issues or had a good reason for voting for either candidate. It is your responsibility to be an informed member of society. As a physician in your community, you will be asked your opinions. Often, right or wrong, they will be listened to and even valued.

The Interview Day
Beginning the Day

The day of your interview has finally arrived. You are tense and nervous. Now what should you do? Take a long shower. Wash your hair. Do some stretching exercises and try to relax. Look in the mirror and say out loud, "I have a lot to offer! I am great! I look great!" (or will, after you shave, put on makeup, or whatever you need to do!) Be positive. Be confident. Put on some exhilarating music while you get ready for your day.

Should you eat before your interview day begins? YES! If you are not hungry due to anxiety, just have a small glass of juice and piece of toast. Do not load up on coffee. You will be wired enough without it. You don't want to add to the shakes you already may have.

Your appearance is important. You need to look fresh, clean, and professional. I think it is very important to be yourself. But you may need to *compromise* just a bit.

For women only. You need to go lightly on the makeup. If you never wear makeup, don't start today. But if you always wear heavy eye shadow and the brightest lipstick you can find, you may need to tone it down. The key is to look like a colleague, not someone going bar hopping. Tie your hair back if it is long, so you don't play or fuss with it during the day. Whether it is long, short, straight, or curly, your hair should be clean, neat, and freshly combed. Today is not the day to try a new hair style. The key is neat and professional, not wild and crazy.

You do not have to wear a dark suit and white blouse. You may look horrible in black or navy. There is nothing wrong with other colors. What is your favorite color? In what do you feel best? Wear that one! Everyone gets tired of seeing plain navy-blue suits sitting across from them during interviews. If you do choose to wear a dark color, there is nothing wrong with adding a colorful blouse, scarf, or simple jewelry. Be yourself!

If you love long, polished nails, that is fine. However, today is not the day to wear your most flamboyant color. Tone it down to a neutral one. You want to go into medicine, not modeling.

For men only. Clean, neat, and professional is the look you need to portray. You do not have to go out and buy a dark suit. Admissions interviewers are well aware that many applicants are on a very tight budget. Some type of jacket, with a shirt and tie, is appropriate. I personally love colorful and bright ties. If you like to add a little spice to your attire, go ahead. If you have a beard or mustache, you do not need to shave it off! Be yourself, but be neat. A trim might be in order. Don't go overboard with jewelry. If you usually wear an earring, go ahead if you wish. The most important points to remember concerning your appearance are to be yourself and to be neat, clean, and professional.

What Does this Day Entail?

Every medical school has a different approach to the applicant's interview day. Some schools invite you for an interview, give you a time and place, and send you off to the interviewing faculty members for an hour or two. As mentioned previously, some schools will do regional interviews and you will meet your interviewer at a specified place off the campus. Other schools will have a complete day arranged for you. During this day you will be given your interview schedule along with a schedule of events. These events may include discussions with current medical students, a talk by faculty or admissions administrators, a breakfast or a lunch, and usually a tour of the medical school's campus and facilities. You may be allowed to visit a lecture or laboratory session, or invited to attend a seminar. Be sure to participate in all activities made available for you. Check out the facilities. What are you looking for? A new modern facility with large, spacious classrooms. Old brick, ivy covered buildings? Research space? Workout facilities? What is the hospital like? Are your clinical clerkships in one hospital or many area hospitals? Talk to your tour guides. Ask lots of questions. Most tour guides are first- or second-year medical students and will answer your questions freely and honestly. *One of your main jobs during this day is to find out everything you need to know in order to decide whether or not you want to go to this particular medical school.*

It is of utmost importance that you talk to people. Talk, ask questions, talk, and ask more questions. You need to communicate freely with students, faculty, and administrators. These people are fountains of information. This is your only opportunity to see the campus and meet people before you have to decide about spending the next four years of your life there. This can be a tough decision if you are one of the lucky people who receive multiple acceptances from several medical schools. Always keep in mind that medical schools are looking for good, solid, quality students. They need students! Try to make this day an enjoyable experience and have fun!

Your second job during this day is to help your interviewers decide whether or not to accept you into their medical program. You will probably have two separate interviews unless it is a panel interview. You need to share information and experiences with your interviewer freely.

The Actual Interview

Here is a small list of cardinal rules that I feel are essential to follow during your interview day:

1. Be on time.

2. Be honest and ethical at all times.

3. Know yourself and maximize your strengths.

4. Be courteous, respectful, and friendly.

5. Show sincere interest in the school.

Your interviewer, whether male, female, black, white, faculty member, or student deserves your respect. Address your interviewer as "Doctor." More often than not, your interviewer will have an M.D. or a Ph.D. Wear a watch or timepiece that you are able to unobtrusively monitor. Do not be late. If you are on a tour, for example, don't be afraid to inform the guide that you have an interview at a particular time. It is *your* responsibility, not the guide's, to keep an eye on the clock. It may be that your interviewer is running late, but be on time anyway. These are very busy people who are spending valuable hours of their time with you because they are care about who is applying to their medical school.

When your interviewer or a secretary calls your name, respond immediately. Look directly into the eyes of your interviewer. As you are being introduced, offer your hand in a hardy handshake. Be firm and confident, not lifeless or bonecrushing. I personally dislike shaking someone's hand who does not respond. This is as important for women as for men. You need to be comfortable offering your hand in a firm handshake.

As you step into your interviewer's office, take a deep breath and sit in the seat offered to you. Try to relax and be yourself. Remember, you have practiced and prepared. This is it!

Your interview will be a conversation between two people. However, the interview will differ from a conversation in that it has a distinct purpose, clear goals, and a set plan. Your interviewer will be fulfilling two tasks: observing everything about you, and asking questions to learn as much as possible about you. Most physicians and professors are trained in interviewing skills and in careful perception of their interactions with people. They will be observing your body language, your appearance, what you do with your hands, the way you articulate, the manner in which you answer or ask questions, your responses to questions, your facial expressions, and your personal warmth and friendliness. Keep in mind that the interview is the humanizing part of the whole admissions process.

Let's go back to my cardinal rules. Number 2. Be honest and ethical at all times. Never say anything that is not true or that you don't wholeheartedly believe in. If you are not interested in primary care, don't say you are. Don't say that your goal is to set up a free clinic in Zimbabwe for the native Africans if your real goal is to set up a group practice in La Jolla, California specializing in plastic surgery. Don't talk about the hours you have spent volunteering with homeless people if, in reality, you only donated last week's lunch money to the clinic. Be honest about your accomplishments. Be honest about your failures. Your interviewer is a real person who has known both success and failure in her life. If your interviewer asks why you received a D in physics, say truthfully that you were having boyfriend troubles. Don't say you caught mononucleosis or were in the midst of a cancer scare instead! Get the picture? Respond appropriately if you are questioned about your MCAT scores. Don't make a lot of excuses for yourself if you did not do well. Believe me, we've heard them all before! Merely state simple facts that are true. Perhaps you had not yet finished the organic chemistry sequence or do not perform well on standardized exams. You can always ask your interviewer if she would advise that you retake the exam. Your straightforwardness and honesty will be noted and appreciated. Not being completely truthful will only get you into trouble.

Number 3: Know yourself and maximize your strengths. Remember all the preparation you did? Research, journaling, talking with others, self-evaluation? Now is the time you will use this information to your advantage. If your interviewer seems to lack direction, be quietly assertive. Lead the discussion into an area you would like to discuss. Say, "Let me give you an example of that" or "Let me share with you an experience I had" or "My mentor (professor, friend, mother, father) always told me...." There may be aspects of your life, past experiences, or personal qualities that you want to make sure you get across to your interviewer. If a door hasn't been opened for you, go ahead and open it yourself. If you are asked about your weaknesses, don't be afraid to admit them. Don't be afraid to laugh at yourself or admit a negative quality. You can mention ways that you have worked to correct or improve on your faults. You can try to turn it into a positive.

My fourth rule is: Be courteous, respectful, and friendly. Be sure to *listen carefully* while your interviewer speaks. Answer questions directly. Lean forward in your chair. Don't be afraid to maintain eye contact. Get to know your interviewer, as he may turn out to be a friend or mentor if you end up in the first-year class. Don't be afraid to ask questions. Ask her what she likes best about the medical school. Ask him how long he's been there and what keeps him there. Ask if he has a family and if the city is a good place to bring up children. Questions such as these can give you insight into your interviewer as a person and how that particular faculty member feels about the school. My fifth rule goes right along with this: Show sincere interest in the medical school. Your interviewer represents the school, has probably spent many years there, and is loyal to it. Be respectful. Find out answers to your questions. Most faculty members love to talk about the school, their research, teaching, or clinical activities. Take advantage of this, but only if you sincerely want to know.

I am adding a sixth rule to the actual interview itself: Try to bond with your interviewer. Find some common ground. Perhaps you were both hockey players in college or you both love to ballroom dance or you are both ardent baseball card collectors. It is great if you immediately find something that you both share. If that doesn't happen, there are other ways. Open yourself up. Spill your guts. Talk about your most difficult life situation and how it has affected you. Talk about your family. Share an embarrassing moment. Talk and share. Help your interviewer to like you. If you establish a bond, mutual respect, and begin to really like each other, your interviewer will go to bat for you. I can't emphasize this enough. She may be on the admissions committee and, through her discussion, change other committee members to vote for you. Every interviewer will write a report about you and your interview. The difference between an extremely positve interview experience and a negative one will make a significant difference in the final selecton vote. Be likeable. Be honest. Try to make the interview experience an enjoyable one.

Favorite Questions

Every interviewer has a distinct style. One interviewer may want to have a simple conversational dialogue. Another may sit behind a desk asking questions in a very formal manner. A few schools have a small panel of interviewers who take turns asking you questions, and all members listen to your answers and are free to comment upon them. Whatever style an interviewer chooses, you must adapt quickly and be as comfortable and honest in your answers and comments as you can be.

Prior to meeting you, your interviewer has spent time carefully reviewing your entire application, has read all letters of recommendation, and has carefully evaluated your personal statement and grades. She will already have many questions ready for you. Usually the interviewer will first try to make the applicant feel comfortable by asking simple questions about family, undergraduate school, or hobby that the candidate mentioned in the application. As you begin to relax, your interviewer will embark upon the more difficult questions. Through your answers, the interviewer will try to determine your sense of responsibility, your empathy and compassion, your awareness of social and ethical issues, your self-appraisal ability, your communication and people skills, your motivation toward medicine, your honesty and integrity, and your community involvement. That is a lot of information to gain in one hour! The interviewer will also be on the lookout for any negative characteristics, such as anger, arrogance, insensitivity, lack of initiative, lack of warmth, or inability to deal with pressure and stress. Sensing any of these traits will immediately send up a red flag and she will put it into the interview report.

Listed below are some typical questions that may be asked in the interview:

Have you had the experience of a close friend being injured, or a death in your family?

Share with me an experience or event which has helped you mature as a person.

Are you willing to treat a patient dying from AIDS?

Which professor have you liked most, and why?

What in your experience has helped you relate and identify with individuals who are sick or need help?

Please discuss any work experience or health-related experiences you have had.

Describe a personal situation you felt was exceedingly stressful or uncomfortable. How did you handle it?

How did you become interested in medicine?

Have you had a mentor or someone very influential in your life?

Have you worked in research?

What course did you enjoy the most and why?

What do you do with your time when you are not studying?

What do you feel is one of the most significant health care problems in the U.S. today?

What challenges do you think you will face in the practice of medicine during the next twenty years?

What have you done in the area of community service?

Do you think physicians have a responsibility to their community?

How would you deal with a patient who repeatedly fails to follow your medical care plans?

How would you evaluate your strengths and weaknesses?

Do you think you have a realistic view of medical school and life in the field of medicine?

What is the most important thing in your life?

What other career choices have you explored?

How would you deal with a friend who is cheating?

What will you do if you do not get into medical school?

What kind of relationship do you have with your family?

Here are some of my own personal favorite questions:

Hindsight is always 20/20! If you could change anything in your life, any decision you made or path that you followed, what would it be?

Name two things you would want to have with you if you were stranded on a desert island.

Name something that you have done of which you are very proud.

If I were talking with your best friend right now, what would she tell me about you?

What would you most like me to know about you?

What are your opinions on ____? (This is usually concerning some event that is currently in the news. It usually will relate to the field of medicine, such as managed health care or the current state of liability and the malpractice system.)

What Is a Bad Interview?

Why is it that sometimes we can walk out of an interview and feel great? And then there are the other times—the occasions when we know the interview was a total bomb. There are basically two main reasons this *bad* interview happens.

The first reason may be *inadequate preparation*. No interview will go well if you have not made a conscious effort to prepare for it. You must know about the school, be able to compare it with others, and know what aspects are important to you. You also need to fully understand the career you wish to undertake. Don't plead ignorance. It won't work.

The second reason may be that you failed to *listen to the questions*. Don't ramble on and on, providing superfluous information. And don't answer questions that were not asked.

Here is a short list of things NOT to do in an interview:

1. Do not show discouragement.

2. Do not falsify any background information or attempt to be someone you're not.

3. Do not use inappropriate humor. You may think lawyer jokes are funny, but your interviewer's spouse may be one!

4. Never disparage other programs, faculty, administrators, students, or applicants.

Follow Up On Your Interview

It is common courtesy to acknowledge the person or persons who have given up their time to interview you. Every faculty member, administrator, or student who interviews you has an extremely busy schedule. Every minute of their time is valuable. The responsibilities of a faculty member at a medical university are tremendous. You need to sincerely thank the people who have spent time with you, either by phone or by mail. Probably the best way is to write a short note. Again, always be honest. If the school is nice, but is not your first choice for the next four years, don't say it is. If you loved the facilities and people, say so. Be honest and straightforward in all your communications with every medical school. It will always pay off.

A Few Final Notes

Always be positive. Always speak kindly of others. Don't criticize the school. You may be overheard. Don't use foul language at any time. I remember a young man who had just finished an interview with a faculty member in the department of pathology. He was talking about an ex-girlfriend to a friend in the hallway and he happened to call her a "stupid _itch." His interviewer happened to overhear the conversation, and, somewhat concerned, added it to the interview report. We had quite a lively conversation during the next admissions committee meeting concerning several aspects of his personality, choice of words, and attitudes toward women. A remark that seems inconsequential to you may affect an interviewer, faculty member, or student enough to change an initial positive feeling to a very negative one.

Occasionally, there is a problem with an interview. For example, you may be scheduled for an interview with Dr. Jones from 1 P.M. until 2 P.M. Suddenly she is paged for an emergency appendectomy and leaves you sitting in a chair in her office. She has spent only 10 minutes with you! How can an interviewer effectively get to know you and your qualifications in only ten minutes? It is not possible. Be calm and professional and walk back over to the admissions office. Talk to one of the personnel or, better yet, ask to speak with the dean of admissions. She will set up another interview for you, hopefully for that same day. Don't be demanding or inconsiderate. Continue to be calm and professional about the situation. These things happen. It will be taken care of.

Every now and then, other situations may arise. You may feel prejudged or your interviewer may talk only about your MCAT scores. If you can't turn the interview around, when it is over, go talk with the dean of admissions about the circumstances. Tell him you felt you were not given a fair chance. Again, be calm and professional. I once had an applicant arrive at my office door nearly hysterical. I quickly led her into my office, shut the door, put an arm around her shoulder, and talked softly with her while attempting to calm her down. I was scared to death that something horrible had happened, perhaps she'd been molested on our campus! However, with choking sobs she told me she didn't think her interviewer had liked her. She had no specifics, just a feeling. I arranged to interview her myself on another day. Meanwhile, I checked her interview report and, to my surprise, it was good. Nothing that I could identify justified her near hysteria. I was truly concerned about this student's maturity and ability to handle difficult situations. If she reacted in such an extreme manner to a simple interview, how would she handle a failure on an exam, a reprimand in surgery, or multiple trauma in the emergency room? This woman needed a few years of growing up, perhaps working in a hospital situation to see exactly what she was getting into.

So be sure to evaluate your situation carefully. Is it important enough to take to the admissions office? Will it truly affect your application? Are you being hysterical for no good reason? Remember, be positive, professional, and personable from the moment you step foot on the campus until the time you leave.

9

Acceptance, Rejection, and Waiting Lists: How to Respond

"You are on the road to success if you realize failure is only a detour."   C. Ten Boom

You have completed the entire application process and applied to a number of medical schools. You have interviewed at the schools you were either very interested in or who invited you. You have sent out notes to the people who took time to interview you. Now what?

Wait! I know it is hard to wait. You are tired of the process and eager to make plans for your next four years. You want to think about financial aid, where to live, and what books to buy. You are impatient to know. This is your future at stake! If you are really going nuts, give the admissions secretary a call. She may be able to give you an idea when final decisions will be made or when letters are to be sent. However, do strive for control. Do not call every other day, or every week. Everyone in admissions is exceptionally busy during this period of time. I remember well the dizzying number of phone calls I would receive weekly. Most often, I would have no information yet to give the caller. Everyone understands your anxiety, but remember we need to use our time efficiently so that we can get the results to you as soon as possible. Daily phone calls lead to valuable time not being used sensibly.

You must also *be aware of the earliest date that your schools send out their acceptance letters*. If you are panic-stricken at the end of January, call the school, and then discover that the school offers no acceptances until March 15, you'll feel pretty silly.

Finally the day comes! You receive an official-looking white envelope showing the return address of one of the medical schools where you interviewed. You slowly tear open the envelope, holding your breath. What is in that letter? There are three possibilities: you are accepted, you are put on a waiting list, or you are rejected.

I'm Accepted!

You have just opened the letter and you have been accepted to enter next year's medical class! Congratulations! You hop around, yelling, telling everyone you grab that your future as a doctor is now an actuality! As the reality of the situation sets in, you need to do some evaluating.

Is this school your number one choice? If it is, great! You need to reply immediately. Usually there will be a form accompanied by your acceptance letter. Sign it. Then check to see if there is an initial fee that you must send in. This fee will vary from school to school. Sometimes there is no fee to hold a place in the class. The AAMC recommends that deposits from accepted students not exceed $100.

You liked the school and would be happy to attend there, but it's not your number one choice. An applicant should be given 2 weeks to respond to an acceptance. During these couple of weeks, you may receive additional letters of acceptance. If this happens, you can go ahead and accept the school of your choice. If the two weeks are up, I would recommend going ahead and signing the letter of intent and paying the school's required deposit. This deposit may be refunded if you decline your acceptance prior to May 15.

If the school is low on your priority list, you need to decide whether to go ahead and take the slot. If you receive no other acceptances, that school may be your only bet. Unless you are very sure of additional acceptance letters coming in, my advice would be to send in your acceptance.

Responsibilities of the Medical Schools

Medical schools have various admissions procedures. There are some medical schools which are on a rolling admissions program. These schools will periodically offer seats in their next year's class as the admissions committee meets and accepts qualified students. In this case, you may have an interview on January 19 and three weeks later receive a letter of acceptance or rejection. Or you may have a very early interview, for example in late October, and receive an acceptance letter on November 14. Schools on a rolling admissions program will continue offering places in their first-year class until the class is filled. If an accepted student rejects the offer, the school will offer an acceptance to the next person on their list. The earliest date that a school begins offering acceptances is October, and the latest date is March 15. Some schools may, however, set their earliest acceptance in December, January, or February.

Other medical schools, though, are not on a rolling admissions program, and release *all* their acceptance letters on a specific date, usually March 15. You, as an applicant, are given a certain number of days or weeks to accept an offer, and an acceptance fee may or may not be needed. The deposit can be up to $100. Most schools will refund your deposit until May 15. After that, the school may keep your deposit as a late withdrawal fee. If you matriculate at that school, the fee is usually credited to your tuition.

After May 15, an applicant may have less than 2 weeks to respond. Schools are actively seeking responses in order to fill their quota. Students still have the freedom to withdraw, however, at any point.

AAMC has a list of recommendations for medical school adherence. Although each school has its own particular schedule of acceptance proce-dures, most institutions abide by these few rules:

- No offers should be made prior to October 15 (except, of course, the early decision programs).

- All offers to applicants should be made by March 15 of the year of matriculation. The number of offers must be equal to the number of students in the first year class.

- After May 15, each medical school is free to contact those students who are holding more than one place and request a decision.

Each school has computer printouts of the names of students who hold an acceptance. Often, students will accept more than one offer. This is referred to as holding multiple acceptances. Unless the applicant has noti-fied the schools and discussed reasons, but May 15 the school is entitled to contact that person. If the first day of classes begins before August 1, the school may contact an applicant prior to May 15, but not before April 15.

Responsibilities of the Acceptee

You, as an applicant, also have specific responsibilities to both the medical school to which you have applied and to other applicants. Five of those responsibilities follow.

Always respond promptly to any correspondence. Be considerate of the schools and other applicants. If your acceptance letter allows you a specific time to answer, please comply. The average response time is two weeks. It may be as long as four weeks. As soon as you make your decision, yea or nay, answer!

If you telephone your response, always follow with a letter. Written communication is always best. I do recall situations in which an acceptance letter was delayed in the mail. I remember one student who desperately wanted to attend medical school in his home town. His wife had a good job, they had just had a baby, and child care was already arranged. He received his letter the day after his response deadline! Of course the dean of admissions understood, and verified his acceptance over the phone. So always call immediately if there is any problem. Admissions people will always take your particular circumstances under consideration. But follow with written verification, along with your deposit.

Candidates are obligated to hold no more than one acceptance at a time. If you are one of the lucky ones to have multiple acceptances, congratulations! However, you are obliged to make a decision and choose the school you wish to attend as soon as possible. Once you decline the other offers, the school is free to make a bid to another applicant. Be considerate and empathetic of others who are in the same situation as you the day before! By May 15, all people who have multiple acceptances *must choose one school and withdraw from the others*.

Promptly withdraw your application from all other schools when you make your final acceptance decision. When you decline an offer, a slot is opened for another anxious applicant. Also, every medical school wants to fill its first-year class as soon as possible. The closer it is to the starting date of classes, the more difficult it is to fill a place just vacated.

Be sure to keep the medical schools informed of any address change. If you will be away from home, or in another country, leave a name and address of a contact person. This will avoid any unnecessary delays in communication.

Deferment

You have been accepted. You have sent your deposit and letter of intent to the school of your choice. Everything is all set. And suddenly....disaster strikes! A family member falls ill, your spouse is accepted to law school across the country, or you are in an automobile accident. You never know what can happen. If there is a good reason why you cannot matriculate that summer or fall, you can request a deferment. I remember an incident where an accepted applicant called only weeks before classes were to begin. Her father had been diagnosed with cancer, was undergoing difficult treatment, and she was the sole care-provider. She asked for a year deferment. Of course this was granted to her. In fact, her father was still ill the following year and she requested a second year deferment. This was also granted to her. Once you are accepted, medical schools will usually do anything within their power to help you and comply with your requests.

I'm Stuck on a Waiting List!

You're not accepted, but you're not rejected. You are on the waiting list. This is both good news and bad news. The good news is: all is not lost! You still may start medical school this year. The bad news is: your life is on hold. For weeks. Maybe months. It is a difficult time for you when you are in limbo. Financial aid applications are due. You may need to relocate if you're finally accepted. You may need to give notice if you have a job. Life becomes even more difficult. Every admissions dean and all the office workers are well aware of how difficult this is for you. But each one of them has limited control over the situation. They, too, are waiting to hear from accepted applicants. A person on the waiting list can't be offered a place until someone accepted declines. The only thing you can do is BE PATIENT. After the deadline of May 15 passes, each school is free to contact the people holding multiple acceptances and request a decision.

It is possible to receive an acceptance call as late as the day after classes begin! To give you an example, I remember a time when a student did not show up for registration. This opened up a spot in the first-year class— and one very happy person hopped a plane in record time!

In the event that one school has offered you an acceptance but you're on a waiting list for a more favored one, this is your call. You can always accept the position and later withdraw. But always be courteous and withdraw as soon as you are notified. You may, however, lose your deposit money.

Don't be afraid to keep in touch with schools when you are on the waiting list. They do like to know that you are still interested in them. Just don't make a nuisance of yourself and call every day.

I've Been Rejected! Now What?

The worst has happened. You have received a letter from the last of the 25 schools where you have applied. It is a "Thanks for applying but…no thanks" letter. You are devastated. What should you do next?

Well, what are your options? First, reevaluate your situation. Do you really want to be a physician or was a parent the one who was pressuring you? Your first decision to make is to choose one of two paths: You can try again, or you can go with an alternative plan already set. You basically have three options here: choose another career altogether or pursue a different aspect of the medical field; apply again; apply to a foreign medical school.

Choose Another Career

When you are in a situation where you must rely on someone else to decide your future, you should always have a contingency plan. Perhaps you have other interests besides medical school. Becoming a science professor, or a researcher, or physical therapist. Not putting all your eggs in one basket is always a good idea. So go on and pursue your next goal and be happy!

You may have talents outside medicine, in theater, the arts, or music. Your second choice may be to pursue your dreams in one of these areas.

Apply Again

But there is also nothing wrong in trying again. Use the knowledge and experiences you have gained from the application process, interviewing, and talking with students and faculty to apply again. I know the whole process is tedious, but you must start all over—from the application itself to references to personal statements to interviews. But remember—you have an advantage this time around. Make sure you improve your application, add and subtract information, and use what you have learned. These suggestions may help.

Try for early decision next year. If you know which school is your first choice, apply to the Early Decision Program. If you don't make it through this program, then send out all the rest of your applications. This gives you two chances.

Improve your application. Take additional courses, such as bio-chemistry, physiology, embryology, or vertebrate anatomy. Demonstrate to the admissions committee that you can handle difficult courses. Retake the Medical College Admissions Test if your scores were low. Raising your scores can be very significant in committee members' eyes.

Get in touch with people who can give you feedback. Seek honesty. What are their suggestions for improving your application? Grades or MCAT scores? Is your maturity in question? Do you need to gain worldly experience? Do you need to gain experience in a hospital setting? Be sure to make an appointment and talk with the admissions dean.

Reapply when you are ready. It may take more than one year to make the necessary changes. Remember, it may already be June, and applications for admission may be accepted as early as June 15. It is impossible to improve such things as grades or MCAT scores in this time. When making the decision whether or not to reapply, you must carefully review your motives and your goals. These are some questions you need to ask yourself:

- Is it worth all the time, expense, and energy to apply for a second, third, or even fourth time?
- If you decide not to reapply, will you feel you haven't tried hard enough?
- Did you apply to a sufficient number of schools?
- Did you apply to schools which were too discriminating or selective (as to credentials)?
- Did you apply early enough?

Only if you applied too late, to too few schools, and to too selective of a school should you reapply immediately. If you submit your application for the forthcoming year, be sure to apply early and to at least twenty schools. A medical education is a medical education wherever you go, so don't look down your nose at any local or state school where you may have the best chance of getting in.

Getting into medical school the second time around is usually a little more difficult. Every year there are more and more applicants. The applicant pool on the whole may have better credentials than you can offer. You must really work at improving your numbers. Or improve your application by working in a medical field such as research, or even earning a master's degree. You must do something that will cause the admissions committee to jump up and take notice. Therefore it will take at least a year to achieve this. You need to make sure you are committed to the time, energy, and expense this will take. Good luck!

Apply to Foreign Medical Schools

On the positive side, I know two excellent physicians who were trained in Guadalajara, Mexico. One is now a practicing pediatric pulmonologist and the other is a pathologist, practicing forensic pathology. Both attended the Universidad Autonoma de Guadalajara. Both doctors have great stories to tell about memorizing anatomy or pathology for exams, and the night before, memorizing everything in Spanish! The downside is that there is, and probably always will be, a possibility of prejudice against foreign medical graduates, or FMGs (this name is changing to international medical graduates or IMGs). There is also no guarantee that you will be able to practice medicine in the United States.

Most students who opt for foreign medical study plan to transfer following either their first year or second year. Transferring after completing the first year of study is very difficult, mainly because there are very few openings in U. S. medical schools. You also must be an exceptional student to even consider a transfer. The second option is a better one. Students finish their two basic science years and then sign up for the United States Medical Licensing Examination, Part 1. This is traditionally the most difficult part of a three-part examination, usually taken at the end of the second year. The exam's content deals primarily with basic science material of anatomy, physiology, biochemistry, pathology, pharmacology, and microbiology. If a foreign medical student does well on this exam, that student has the best chance of transferring to an American medical college for the last two clinical years of training.

Be sure to gather as much information about foreign medical training as you can. Get a list of schools from either AMCAS or the World Health Organization. Only you can decide whether or not you have the perseverance, fortitude, and motivation to pursue foreign study. You will be battling a new language, a new culture, and lack of family and friends. If you can, talk to a FMG or a physician who obtained partial training in a foreign medical school. It always helps to have some firsthand information. It may sound glamorous to study on the beach while attending St. Georges Medical School in Grenada. But be aware of all the pros and cons before you commit.

10

How To Be a Successful Student

"Live a balanced life—learn some and think some and draw and paint and sing and dance and play and work every day some."

Robert Fulghum

So many students are petrified as they enter the hallowed halls of medical education. It may be the first time you have seen a cadaver. The workload is overwhelming. Everyone else seems to be studying harder, has a better background (like that one who has a Ph.D. in biochemistry), knows more than you, and seems to have it together. This chapter will deal with the most frequent problems that arise during medical school, suggestions on lifestyle and having a life outside of medicine, and recommendations for seeking help when problems arise.

The Differences Between College and Medical School

You have managed to do well in your education up until now or you wouldn't be contemplating a career in medicine. Good study habits are essential, and hopefully you have mastered them. However, you should be aware of some major differences between undergraduate and graduate education.

The Four Major Differences Between Undergraduate and Graduate Education

In graduate school...
1. There are *massive* amounts of material.
2. There are fewer exams.
3. There are Totally Unfamiliar Materials (TUMs).
4. There is no one to hold your hand.

Let's discuss these differences. First of all, the amount of material you will be expected to know is phenomenal. The subject matter of one day of medical school lectures, labs, and discussion groups is like at least one week of undergraduate classes! So the **First Golden Rule** of medical school is: **DO NOT GET BEHIND.** If you miss one day of the fall quarter, for example, you may miss four hours of gross anatomy lecture, a two-hour biochemistry lecture, and a three-hour gross anatomy dissection laboratory. That is a massive amount of material to catch up on when the next day there are six straight hours of additional lectures, plus a two-hour introduction to clinical medicine class.

A **Second Golden Rule** is this: **DO NOT SKIP ESSENTIAL LEARNING OPPORTUNITIES.** You can't afford to skip classes, or spend a few extra days on vacation, or just sleep in. The faculty members at a medical school all have either M.D.s, Ph.D.s or both. These are people who have spent significant time and effort in preparing lectures, laboratory sessions, discussion groups, and clinical cases through which to learn. You can't waste their time and ask them to review the material with you just because *you* didn't feel like getting out of bed that morning. You must motivate yourself to attend all learning sessions, and be awake and participate in those sessions at all times. You are paying a lot of money for these privileges, and it's up to you to make good use of them. You must constantly keep up with your reading, laboratory sessions, and lecture notes.

The second major difference in medical school is that there are usually fewer exams and quizzes. Your grade may depend on just one or two exams. Or possibly on one written paper. Some course grades may depend only on a midterm and final exam. Some clinical rotations may give one mini-board exam. You fail it, you fail the clerkship!

The third difference is that most of the material will be totally unfamiliar. These are not courses you have taken before. This is not material you just need to freshen up on. Medical school has been compared to learning a whole new language. For example, even a leg is not a leg anymore—it is only the part of the lower limb between the knee and foot. Diseases, drugs, diagnoses, nerves, muscles, biochemical and embryologic structures. This new language has names you're never dreamed of. One student told me that one of the weirdest words she learned in medical school was "syncytiotrophoblast." (Figure that out on your own!) The subject matter for the day's lectures may be totally unfamiliar to you. The only way to keep the TUMs under control is to read ahead. Be prepared and familiar with the lecture material *before* you attend the class. The very least you should do is to skim the material, becoming accustomed to all the new terminology. If you do not do this, especially in subject areas such as embryology and neuroanatomy, you will find yourself totally lost and confused during the lecture hours. Those hours will be wasted, and you cannot afford to waste any time. Therefore, the **Third Golden Rule is**: **BE PREPARED.**

The fourth difference in graduate training is the fact that you, alone, are responsible for your education. There will be no one holding your hand. You are treated like the adult you are. It is your responsibility to go to class, make up material that you miss, be accountable to your lab partners to share the work. Most medical schools are on an honor system. There will be no monitors looking over your shoulder during exams. Faculty members will come and go for questions. You may even take a coffee break if you feel you have the time. The whole idea is that you are responsible and expected to live up to the code of ethics of people in medicine.

So you can see that your years in medical school will be different from your undergraduate years. Let's go on with study suggestions and more Golden Rules.

Study Aids
Form study groups

Right at the start, you need to find a couple of fellow students who would like to be your study partners. In the first-year course, gross anatomy for example, you will usually be assigned four people to a cadaver. If you get along well, you can study together, constantly quiz each other, even set up practice tests for each other. This is a great way to study and to see if you are understanding all the TUMs.

Sometimes the four anatomy lab partners aren't a good mix. So mingle with other people and see if other students may have a similar approach to studying as yours . Choosing a study partner who likes to cram at the last minute is not a good idea if you are a day-to-day plodder. Likewise, deciding upon a study partner who is a night owl will not be conducive to your habit of rising at dawm. Group learning can be very effective, so you don't have to stick with just one study buddy. In a group of three to four, you can assign areas or TUMs for one person to "teach" and explain to the others. This is a great way to learn, because in order to teach a subject you must have first mastered it. Bounce questions off each other, use the new vocabulary, quiz each other. If you don't understand a subject area, most likely someone in the group will. Or better yet, pick that subject to teach the others and figure it out for yourself. This leads us to the next critical point and **Fourth Golden Rule** of medical school: **MANAGE YOUR TIME.**

Time Management

If you have not learned the skill of utilizing your time wisely, you had better do so. Many days you will be attending lectures and participating in laboratory sessions from 8:00 A.M. until 5:00 P.M. You need to add hours of study time in your day, plus time out for food, and perhaps a little recreation. You must plan your day. You must get organized. Get yourself a daily calendar with lots of space for writing and write everything down. There is simply too much to remember, so if you don't write it down, you'll forget it. Don't waste time, either. If a professor doesn't show up for lecture (this is rare in medical school), use the extra hours for study or to read the material for the next day. Go out for a half-hour jog at lunch time and clear your mind. Or do an errand or two so you don't have to do them during your evening study hours. If you do not utilize your time wisely, you will soon find yourself exhausted, unhappy, and totally overwhelmed. This leads us to the next point and **Fifth Golden Rule**: **DO NOT PANIC.**

Do Not Panic

In a new situation, bogged down with too much to do, too little time, lack of sleep and good nutrition and exercise, you can lose control of your emotions. Particularly during exam times, you can feel on the verge of a breakdown. With books, notes, atlases, papers, and diagrams in front of

you, panic strikes. Panic stricken, you begin frenzied and inefficient studying. The more inefficient you are, the more panic you feel, and it all turns
into a vicious cycle. It is a horrible feeling that I remember well. The day
before my very first gross anatomy written exam and lab practical, I
panicked. In a total fit of hysteria, I went from subject to subject, tearing
at books, memorizing facts, forgetting everything. Crying. Sobbing. After
staying up most of the night, I started the anatomy practical exam utterly
exhausted, red- and bleary-eyed, and still in a panic. Almost crazed, I went
from cadaver to cadaver, trying to find something I remembered. When
the exam was over, I cried. I knew I had flunked. Well, the final result was
that I received a 69 percent. In order to pass, you needed a 70 percent.
Now that I look back and have had the experience of being a professor
for over a decade, that exam grade really wasn't so bad. Usually there are
three to four exams, maybe more, during this course. It is pretty easy to
raise your grade by just doing a little better on the next exam. Following
that exam, I realized I could not allow myself to get into that nightmarish
panic again. I learned to keep those feelings under control.

If you find this happening to you, first accept the situation. Then push
yourself away from your desk and leave the library, your apartment, or
wherever you are studying. Take a walk. Get some exercise. Throw the
ball to your dog. Just do something that frees your mind for a few minutes
until you begin to think rationally again. Remember, it is only a test. You
will not die. Your life will not be over if you do not perform well. Put the
situation into perspective. Once you go back to your studying, divide the
subject matter into small chunks. Take one bit at a time. Review. Do not
let your mind wander into all the other chunks of material you have to
master. Force your mind onto only the one area. Keep your emotions
under control and take it one step at a time. Only when you're ready, go
on to the next. Slowly you will master one set of information at a time
and you will become better at focusing on one tree instead of the huge
entire forest!

Support Systems

Medical school is a time of stress, hard work, and many challenges. It can
be all-encompassing and sometimes isolating while you are immersed in
so much work. Therefore, it is very important to have your own support
systems. You need people with whom you can open up and share feelings.

There can be times when you are fearful of failure, convinced you'll never make it, or wanting to say "I quit." Talking it out will help.

You need to trust the people you share this with, and choose good listeners. You don't want to be sharing your deepest fears with a friend while they are looking at their watch every two minutes!

Your support systems can include parents or siblings. These people are closest to you, know your faults, and love you anyway. You will be amazed at how empathetic your own parents can be if you give them a chance.

A significant other, be it spouse or friend, can be a tremendous source of comfort. If this person is in medicine also—great. He will be particularly sensitive to your needs. If she works or goes to school outside the medical field, this is also great, in a different way. You can separate yourself from medical school and immerse yourself in another world for a while. It is a hazardous situation when your significant other is outside medicine. That person can feel very left out. You are learning a new world and vocabulary. It can appear that you are beginning to speak a different language. All of a sudden you feel that your lab partner understands you *so* much better! And you find a relationship developing into more than just a friendship. Be aware that this can happen. And also be aware that this situation you're in (medical school) is only temporary, as are your feelings for your colleague. Your colleague doesn't really understand you better than your significant other. It only appears so temporarily. So don't fall into this trap! It will only add more stress to your life.

A support system can also be in the form of a professor or dean. Many students form special mentor-like relationships with a faculty member at their medical college. This relationship can be a source of learning and encouragement for both professor and student. I have formed many special relationships with former students during my academic years. Certain students have sought me out for conversations, advice, and assistance in problems, both personal and academic. These relationships have been some of my most rewarding experiences as both a teacher and dean. So never be afraid to talk to a faculty member. Some may seem unapproachable or uninterested in medical students, so choose someone who appears kind and concerned. You won't be sorry.

Some schools, or their student affairs or student services departments, arrange for special mentorships for students during their first year. Please take advantage of this program if your school has one. Certain programs will hook up a faculty member with several students. Meetings can either be individual or with the whole group. These group sessions may turn into gripe sessions, but often they're very informative and helpful. Other programs deal with a "big brother/big sister" approach. Each first-year student is matched up with a second-year student who knows the ropes. Second-year students generously share books, lecture notes, and advice with their partner. Sometimes these partnerships develop into lifelong friendships.

Last of all, don't forget your spiritual support. Don't forsake your religion just because you think you're too busy. Whether you are Christian, Catholic, Buddhist, Hindu, or other, you need to spend a little time away from the hustle and bustle of your daily schedule. Working out a time for prayer or meditation, whether on a daily or weekly basis, is essential for a healthy spiritual life and can be a great source of strength.

The important point is to utilize and develop the support systems available to you. This is the **Sixth Golden Rule**: **DEVELOP SUPPORT SYSTEMS.** These support systems will be a source of sustenance and encouragement throughout your medical school career.

Help!

During your four years of medical school you will be memorizing large volumes of information. You'll be dealing with new situations every day. You will be spending much time in what appears to be a threatening environment. There will be a heavy workload, anxiety, lack of free time and sleep. Sometimes this can lead to depression. There will be times during these years when you will need to seek help. This is the **Seventh Golden Rule**: **SEEK HELP WHEN YOU NEED IT.** Some of these situations will be academic, others will be personal.

Academic Problems

These can arise at any time during your basic science years (the first two years) or your clinical years (years 3 and 4). But these problems are particularly prevalent during the first year of medical school. With massive amounts of material that is totally unfamiliar, it's no wonder that first year students find themselves in academic difficulty.

The most common academic problem we see in medical students is failing grades in gross anatomy. This is a traditionally difficult subject, mainly because of the huge amounts of daily material and time-consuming laboratory sessions several times per week. It is so easy to get behind. By the time most students realize they are in difficulty, they have already failed the midterm. This leaves one final exam to pull their grade up to a passing one.

So first of all, take advantage of quizzes, if they are given. If you fail the first one, seek help. Catch your mistakes early. Discover where you're going wrong. The biggest mistake failing students make is to not seek help early enough. Put your pride aside and don't be embarrassed to admit you are failing. There are many professors who are willing to spend extra time with students in trouble.

Second, don't forget about your fellow students. Some may have had previous courses and can be a great source of study help. Most students are willing to share their knowledge. Seek out students you know are doing very well and find out their study techniques. It's not hard to discover who the top students are. Gossip runs rampant in medical schools.

If you are having difficulty in a clinical rotation, first evaluate your approach. Are you dressed appropriately, wide-eyed and eager? Do you ask appropriate questions? Are you on time or ahead of schedule? Do you attend all rounds and appear interested? Do you take advantage of all the lectures and seminars? Are you reading every night in your subject area, looking up the problems your patients are having? Are you utilizing any free time to study for your mini-board examination? If you can say yes to all these questions, then you should first seek help from a friendly intern or first-year resident who is interested in teaching medical students. Even if you are not assigned to work with that particular resident, follow her around. Pick her brain. Find out the most important things to learn on that particular service. Another option is to seek some help from a fellow student who has done well in that particular rotation. Just having been through the clerkship, he may offer some very useful tidbits.

Personal Problems

You will encounter personal problems throughout life, whether you're in medical school or not. Being in medical school sometimes just seems to breed trouble. Dealing and coping with serious problems of any kind is beyond the scope of this book, but I will just mention briefly the types of personal problems I have encountered.

The number one problem is dealing with failure. The fear of failure. Actually failing courses. Being asked to leave medical school. Of feeling that you are not good enough. These feelings lurk in the heart of many medical students. You are not alone.

The actual act of failing something, an exam or course, is sometimes easier to deal with than the fear it might happen. First, you must understand that fearing failure is totally nonproductive. It actually makes you live through failure twice. The first is living through the failure in your mind. The second time is when it actually happens. Put the possibility of failure out of your mind, and deal with it only if and when it happens.

Don't forget there are many people in a medical setting to help you. Every school has personnel in their student services or student affairs office. If your problem is beyond their scope, they will refer you elsewhere. There are trained psychologists and psychiatrists who work with students. Utilize these facilities. And always remember there are people to help you and you are not the first student to be in this situation.

Depression can also be a problem for medical students. Everyone gets down now and then, but if the feelings persist and begin affecting your sleep and eating habits, seek help. Don't hesitate and don't be embarrassed. More people are walking around hospitals on antidepressant medication than you think. And they're not patients.

Finally, I've seen many relationship problems. Spouses, friends, and families of medical students often aren't aware of the work involved in being a medical student. Don't let these problems percolate. Go talk to someone—colleague, professor, dean. Talking always helps. Others can look at the subject more objectively. If your problems don't improve, don't hesitate to seek counseling.

Is There Life Outside Medicine?

There is life outside of medicine, but it is up to you to want it and make it happen. People are creatures of habit. Many little parts of your life, such as meals, are just naturally worked into your schedule. If you want a life outside of medicine, you need to first schedule those activities into your busy day. After a certain period of time, they will develop into a part of your life. Ask anyone who has led a sedentary life and added an exercise program to their routine. It's a chore a first. You might not always be in the mood. But after a few weeks, months, even years, you just naturally go for that jog or work out at the health club.

Different forms of exercise are a great way to relieve stress, make new friends, and feel better about yourself. Take up racquetball, tennis, or golf. Most people love to smack little balls around. If this helps your tension, great. I've also known medical students and physicians to learn to ballroom dance. This activity kills several birds with one stone. It is good exercise. You can do it with your significant other, so you add quality time with your sweetheart. And you meet a whole new group of people who are rarely involved in medicine. It's hard to think about what's going on at the hospital when you're trying to remember how to do a complicated fox-trot step. So in general, you really need to add physical activity that can blend into your lifestyle.

Relationships are, to me, the most important key to a healthy and happy life. Family and friends need constant nurturing. Special relationships can begin to fall apart without time and a little effort spent on them. Spouses, significant others, and children add so much dimension. It's hard to be a whole person without these caring relationships. On a recent episode of the hit television show, "ER," a husband and father lay dying from a heart condition. What this patient regretted the most was the lack of time he spent with his young daughter. He asked for her and held her close as he passed away. It was a tear-jerking scene. All too often situations like this happen in our crazy, get-ahead world. Not many people, on their deathbed, have said, "If only I spent more time at the office."

Adding a creative outlet is great therapy for a person involved in medicine. I know a pediatric otolaryngologist who absolutely loves to garden. His yard is a masterpiece of rare flowers, shrubs, and trees. At almost every time of the year there is something blooming in his gardens. He is the neighborhood expert on plants, and gives advice to anyone who asks for it.

I've also known physicians who were tap dancers, painters, musicians, and writers. Their hobbies add a special character to them, their patients, and their lives.

Getting involved with a spiritual or religious community is another way to have a part of yourself outside medicine. This group can support joy, peace, and spirituality in your daily life. As you are dealing with both life and death, it is very natural to bring this sense of spirituality to your office and patients. It can be a tremendous source of comfort.

The more facets of your life you develop, the more you will bring to medicine and your patients.

Keep Things in Perspective

During the craziness of medical school—the exams, the patients, the papers, and research—you need to keep everything in perspective. Sometimes you will need to focus only on learning and to appreciate the vast amount of knowledge you are accumulating. **Don't focus so heavily on grades**. Remember the old joke, "What do you call the person who finished last in his medical school graduating class?" Answer: "an M.D." It's true. Not everyone can be first or second. Many schools have gone to a Pass/Fail grading system to alleviate some of the stress and competition. I'm certainly not saying that grades are not important. They are. Particularly if you are interested in going into a highly competitive residency at a high-powered medical center. But don't focus on grades to the exclusion of all else. Medical schools offer so many fantastic learning opportunities. Get involved in research, missions, homeless clinics, and early clinical work. As you develop other skills, you'll focus less on grades.

A second important point is this: **Don't be too hard yourself.** Sometimes we can be our own worst enemies. Sit back and contemplate for a moment what you have achieved and the goals you have met. Maybe you flunked microbiology. Okay, so you'll need to spend some time remediating, or take the course over. Relax—this isn't a race. Accept the fact and go on and make the most of it. Don't keep kicking yourself and telling yourself you won't make it or you won't get into a residency. Be kind to yourself.

Always give yourself alternatives and second chances and don't put all your eggs in one basket. For example, when you take an exam, simply do your best. If you fail, see where you went wrong. You always have a chance to improve your grade with another exam. Or if you do fail the course, remember that the school will not just kick you out. There can be make-up exams or remedial courses in the summer so you don't lose a year. If all else fails, you may lose a year but they still won't kick you out. You have quite a number of chances before that ever happens. So, lighten up and don't put so much stress on yourself.

A third point is this: **Enjoy the journey.** Wayne W. Dyer said, "Success is a journey, not a destination." This is a wise attitude. Medical school is a journey you're on to fulfill your dream of working as a physician and healer for the rest of your life. You'll get there soon enough. Enjoy the freedom to learn. Enjoy just being a student, without too many responsibilities. School is a cocoon, and you'll be out in the real world soon enough. Relish the camaraderie of your classmates. These are your fellow colleagues, and in the future you'll be referring patients to each other and continuing your relationships. Enjoy those smelly times in the gross lab with your partners, where you have the fantastic opportunity to spend hours of time trying to understand the miracle of the human body. And bless those interns and residents and attending physicians who have the final responsiblility for those patients whose symptoms have completely baffled you!

Finally, **preserve your outside interests.** Spend time away from medicine. You can't put things into perspective if you don't immerse yourself in something different from time to time. I've talked about this previously, that you must have a part of your life away from medicine. Keep a positive outlook. You have a great career ahead of you.

As you begin your new career, let me review one more time:

The Eight Cardinal Rules of Being a Medical Student
1. Do Not Get Behind.
2. Do Not Skip Essential Learning Opportunities.
3. Be Prepared.
4. Manage Your Time.
5. Do Not Panic.
6. Develop Support Systems.
7. Seek Help When You Need It.
8. Get a Life.

11

Making the Most of Your Residency

"I do not simply want to spend my life, I wish to invest it."

Helen Keller

You have already decided that you want to be a doctor. Great! But that is only the first step. You have another major decision to make by the beginning of your fourth year in medical school. And that is: "What specialty shall I choose?" The area of specialty you select will determine the types of patients you see, your workload, your income, and perhaps your eventual geographical location. You have a lot of soul searching to do. The selection of a specialty is a very complex, individual decision. In several surveys, 27 percent of students have made that decision prior to entering medical school. However, more times than not, the student will change his or her mind during the time of clinical rotations. The final decision will be based on personality traits, academic ability, age, sex, marital status, economic factors, role models, clinical experience, even race and socioeconomic status. This chapter will also explain the National Residency Matching Program (NRMP), the Couples Match, the Unmatch Day, and Match Day.

Residency Facts

A residency is a hospital-based program that trains a physician in a particular area of medicine. It usually consists of three to seven years of training following medical school. For example, if you want to be a family practitioner, you will have three years of additional school or training before you actually hang out your shingle. On the other hand, if you have always wanted to be a surgeon specializing in hand surgery, you will spend three to five years in a general surgery residency, two years in a plastic surgery residency, and an additional one year in a hand surgery program. Under these circumstances, you would be spending a possible twelve years of training post-college before you open your surgical practice.

Every medical graduate who wants to practice medicine must graduate from a residency program. You need one year of residency or *internship* to obtain a medical license. Your residency years should be a great time in your life. You are a doctor, you care for patients, but you do not have the full responsibility for their welfare. There is always an attending physician above you. You also get paid for what you do. Unfortunately, considering the hours you have to work, the actual hourly pay can be as little as one dollar per hour, as one complaining resident told me. Salaries range from $30,000 to $40,000 per year. But money shouldn't be the goal here. You are learning your life's work.

The years of residency training are very demanding. You work long and hard hours. For many years, residents were known to work forty hours without a break. Being on call every other night was the norm. If you worked fewer than 100 to 150 hours a week you were considered a total wimp. In the last few years, medical educators have begun to realize that this workload is detrimental to both the patients and the resident's learning process. The state of New York actually passed a law that limits the hours a resident is allowed to work to 80 hours. Most programs do comply with new standards and state laws.

What Are Specialties and Subspecialties?

A *specialty* is an area of medicine limited to a particular field. A specialist is a physician whose practice is limited to a particular branch of medicine or surgery. The specialist has had advanced training and is certified by a specialty board.

Family medicine, internal medicine, and pediatrics are considered to be the three *primary care* specialties. At the present time, these areas of medicine are in need of physicians. Other specialties are more limited and specific in scope, such as ophthalmology, otolaryngology (ENT), and cardiology.

Subspecialists are more specialized than the specialists. For example, specialists in internal medicine are considered to be either general internists or subspecialists in internal medicine. Subspecialties in internal medicine include: allergy and immunology, cardiology, clinical pharmacology, critical care, gastroenterology, geriatrics, infectious disesase, rheumatology, hematology, oncology, endocrinology and metabolism, nephrology, pulmonology, and clinical nutrition.

There are currently 69 areas of specialization in medicine:

Aerospace Medicine
Allergy and Immunology
Anesthesiology
Blood Banking
Cardiology
Chemical Pathology
Child Neurology
Child Psychiatry
Colon and Rectal Surgery
Critical Care/Anesthesiology
Critical Care/Internal Medicine
Critical Care/Surgery
Dermatology
Dermatopathology
Diagnostic Radiology
Emergency Medicine
Endocrinology and Metabolism
Family Practice
Forensic Pathology
Gastroenterology
Geriatric Medicine
Hand Surgery
Hematology
Immunopathology
Infectious Diseases
Internal Medicine
Medical Microbiology
Musculoskeletal Oncology
Neonatology
Nephrology
Neurological Surgery
Neurology
Neuropathology

Nuclear Medicine
Nuclear Radiology
Obstetrics/Gynecology
Occupational Medicine
Oncology
Ophthalmology
Orthopedic Sports Medicine
Orthopedic Surgery
Otolaryngology
Pathology
Pediatric Cardiology
Pediatric Endocrinology
Pediatric Hematology/Oncology
Pediatric Nephrology
Pediatric Orthopedics
Pediatric Surgery
Pediatrics
Physical Medicine and
    Rehabilitation
Plastic Surgery
Preventive Medicine/General
Psychiatry
Public Health
Pulmonary Diseases
Radiation Oncology
Radioisotopic Pathology
Rheumatology
Surgery, General
Surgery, Thoracic
Transitional Year
Urology
Vascular Surgery

What Is the Match?

The National Residency Matching Program is more commonly known as the *Match*. The majority of fourth-year medical students get their first-year training positions through this method. Simply put, the purpose of the Match is to match medical students with a residency program. Usually in late February of the senior year, students must complete what is called a Rank Order List (ROL). Each student does this on a computer system called the Rank Order List Confirmation and Input System. Using this program, the student ranks the residency programs in order of preference. The student can rank up to fifteen different residency programs. At the same time, each residency program across the country completes a similar computer program, only listing the medical student candidates in the order of that residency program's preference. By this computer system, each student is matched up with a residency program on his or her ROL.

Over the years, this system (which began in 1951) has been able to match most students with slots in the programs that they rank relatively high. As a general rule, approximately 57 percent match with their first choice, 16 percent with their second choice, 10 percent with their third choice, and 11 percent with their fifth or lower choice of program.

Early Matches

Separate matches exist for several of the different specialties. These include neurology, plastic surgery, neurosurgery, ophthalmology, otolaryngology, radiation oncology, and urology. These early match programs require the student to submit their Rank Order Lists (ROL) by mid-January. Deans' offices usually receive the results by the end of January or early February.

Unmatch Day

The worst has happened! At 8:00 P.M. the eve before Unmatch Day, you receive a telephone call from the dean of students. She informs you that you were not matched. Do not panic! This has happened to many students before, it will continue to occur, and it happens whether or not you are a good student.

Unmatch Day is the day before Match Day, usually in mid-March. All the residency programs that have not filled all their positions with the graduating seniors are apprised of their situation. All the students who are not matched are also informed. At noon (EST) what seems like utter chaos begins. Phones are ringing, fax machines are beeping, students are weeping. The best thing to do is to scan the lists of programs that have positions available and begin calling them in the order of your priority and interest. Have all essential materials at your fingertips: transcripts, dean's letter, reference letters, personal statement, and curriculum vitae (or resume). You will need to fax them to the program director. Although it is an extremely stressful few hours, almost all students are matched by the end of the day.

Match Day

The exact dates for the events in the Matching Program change from year to year, but on a specific day in mid-March, the Match results are sent out. All students and programs are notified of the results at NOON (EST). Each student is handed a white envelope that announces where that student will be living and what he or she will be doing for the next three to five years.

This is a tremendously exciting time for the graduating students. Families and friends usually accompany the student to a reception most schools provide. Oftentimes, local news media are present to do interviews with the excited students, faculty, and administrators.

Couples' Match

Today, there are a fair number of medical students who are married, have plans to marry, or are likewise committed to each other. The NMRP, realizing that medical couples were becoming more common, instituted a Couples Match in the early 1990s. This program assists couples in matching to the same geographical location. All of the initial steps of applying to residencies are the same. Each individual signs up for the match, applies and interviews at his or her choice of programs. In December, the couple decides whether or not to commit to the Couples Match. They should, of course, each apply to programs in a particular choice of cities. What good is it if one of the partners interviews at UCLA, and the other half of the couple only applies to programs in the Northeast? There are special worksheets and instructions for the Couples Match, and in January, the partners must decide on combinations of programs which will work for them. For example, Mark wants to go into pediatrics and is interested in several programs in Denver and Boston. Rebecca wants to go into general surgery. She interviews at several programs in the same cities. They get together and rank their programs in the same order. In this way, they increase their chance of being matched together in the same city.

Today's Trends

For the past decade, medical students have been busily pursuing the subspecialties. There are simple reasons for this. First, the reimbursement has been much greater in a subspecialty than in primary care. Medical students have just spent four years in school. They have spent great sums of money on tuition, fees, and books. They have borrowed money from every available source: federal government, state subsidies, Mom and Dad, grandparents, and good old Uncle Pete. They owe thousands and thousands of dollars. With a monthly loan repayment cost that can exceed a typical house payment, is it any wonder that a newly-graduated physician would choose a practice in general surgery with a projected income of over $200,000, rather than a practice in pediatrics that might bring in $70,000 per year?

The second reason is often one of prestige. In the world of medicine, as in general society, there is a type of hierarchy. A cardiac and thoracic surgeon may look down upon the family doc that just referred a patient to him. Sad though it is, the fact remains that surgical specialties and others that require longer and more intense years of study are considered the top of the heap.

The trend toward highly specialized medicine is just beginning to change. More equality in reimbursement and pay scales is a high priority item in medicine today. There is a great need for more physicians in the areas of primary care. In a few instances, there is a special incentive for medical students to choose a residency in family medicine. Sign-on bonuses are given to first-year residents in a few residency programs. The federal government is actually getting involved by offering special financial-aid packages to medical students who commit to primary care medicine early in their medical school career.

Are there residencies that are easier or more difficult for a student to get into? Certainly! Specialties such as dermatology, diagnostic radiology, emergency medicine, otolaryngology, and obstetrics–gynecology are currently the most competitive. However, you must keep in mind that these specialties change with supply and demand. Popularity of a certain specialty is also cyclical. Back in the early 1980s, for example, obstetrics–gynecology was wide open. Anyone who applied could almost be guaranteed a spot in a residency program. For the last couple of years, however, ob–gyn has been highly competitive, and only the most qualified applicants will be lucky enough to gain a position.

Less competitive are fields such as pathology, pediatrics, and psychiatry. But always keep in mind that at any time this can change. Family medicine has been considered one of the easier residencies to get into, but the most recent Match Program showed more and more graduates choosing family medicine. So, who knows, five years from now family medicine may move into the highly competitive ranks and shove dermatology to the back of the line.

You can't try to beat the system or play games with the Match Program. All you can do is work your hardest and make choices as to what *YOU* want to do for the rest of your life.

Financing Your Medical Education
with Deb Heineman, M.A., M.Ed.

"Make yourself necessary to the world and mankind will give you bread."   Ralph Waldo Emerson

How much does medical school really cost? What scholarships and loans are out there? Will I ever be debt-free? The reality of the cost of medical education can be overwhelming. Many medical school applicants have never had to deal with the laborious task of applying for financial aid. This chapter will begin by defining the probable cost of a medical education, and move on to types and sources of financial aid.

You've probably heard that a medical education is a very expensive venture. This is true. You have probably heard of the nightmarish stories of owing hundreds of thousands of dollars at the end of your medical training. You are probably worrying about the affordability of a medical education and being in debt for the rest of your life. These things can happen. On the bright side, however, there are many ways to decrease costs, and help is available. There are obtainable sources of financial aid, and there are ways to manage and control your debt.

The Cost of a Medical Education

Let's begin with the cost of four years of medical school. As you probably know, the price of an education at each of the 125 medical institutions is different. The variables include such things as the type of school (is it private or public?) and the location of the institution. A private medical school education can cost you up to five times more than an education received at a state institution. One year of medical education at the Louisiana State University will cost approximately $4,776, while a private institution down the road at Tulane University School of Medicine will cost $22,311 per year in tuition alone. You'll definitely be paying the price for a private school's education. Another example of the substantial savings of a public education can be found in Illinois. One year at Southern Illinois University School of Medicine will cost about $8,000 compared to $25,000 a year at the Pritzker School of Medicine at the University of Chicago, a private school.

Attending a local school can likewise save you 200–300 percent or more. For example, a resident of Texas will pay approximately $6,000 dollars to attend the medical schools at Texas A & M, Texas Tech, or University of Texas. But a student applying from Indiana will pay around $24,000 for just one year. That's a lot of money for an education! And it is a lot of money saved if you attend a medical school in your state. Let's take another example. The University of North Carolina Chapel Hill School of Medicine's tuition and fees for the year 1992–93 for a resident was $1,622. This compares to the cost for a nonresident of $15,268. What a difference! Obviously, schools in a great location with great weather, sunshine, and beaches, are going to be more desirable than schools located in cold, damp, and dreary climes. But remember, the majority of your time will be spent in classrooms, laboratories, libraries, and hospital rooms, not in parks, beaches, and shopping malls.

Besides tuition and fees, additional living costs will vary from city to city and state to state. A school located in an area of the country where the cost of living is very high will cost you more due to the increased living costs you will incur living there. Another point to consider is the length of the program. As mentioned in Chapter 7, there are several options to the regular program. You may be admitted to a traditional four-year program at one school and offered a five-year flexible curriculum program at another. That additional year will add expenses to the total cost of your medical education.

Direct Educational Costs

You need to know the items that are considered by the finanical aid office when establishing a cost of education for medical students. First, there are *direct costs*. They are called direct costs because they are charged by the school and will be paid by you accordingly. The following are considered to be direct educational costs:

- Tuition

- Nonresident fee (if applicable)

- General/student fees

- Equipment fees

- Course fees

- Insurance (e.g., disability, health, liability)

- Immunizations

Some costs will vary from year to year. For example, the equipment and course fee charges will depend on your year in school and the classes in which you are enrolled. Usually, you will have laboratory fees during your first two years for courses, such as gross anatomy, microanatomy, microbiology, and pathology. During your two clinical years, these particular fees will not apply. Additionally, most medical colleges require students to be covered by a health insurance policy as well as a liability policy. The institution may offer a variety of insurance plans to their students. However, you may already have insurance coverage through a parent or spouse, so you would not be assessed for that particular fee. Usually immunizations for diseases such as hepatitis are also required. If you have proof of prior immunizations, you will not be required to be revaccinated.

Indirect Costs

Indirect educational costs include items such as books and living expenses. These costs include:

- Books and supplies

- Rent

- Utilities

- Food

- Transportation

- Personal/miscellaneous

It is the area of indirect costs where a student can use effective budgeting skills to reduce expenses and therefore spend less than what the financial aid office has estimated for these costs.

Now you know what items are included in the cost of a medical education. So let's look at a sample cost of education for a first-year student attending a public medical school in his or her home state in the midwestern part of the country:

Direct Costs		*Indirect Costs*	
Tuition	$8,700	Rent	$4,200
General fees	220	Utilities	1,800
Equipment Fee	165	Food	3,000
Course Fee	40	Personal	950
Insurance	700	Books/supplies	950
Immunizations	150	Transportation	3,800
Subtotal	$9,885	Subtotal	$14,700
TOTAL COST OF EDUCATION = $25,585			

When you accept a place in the first-year class of a medical school, your direct costs will be fixed. Increases in tuition may sometimes occur, but they shouldn't be too significant. As you can see, over half your cost comes from living expenses. You should consider that you would incur these regardless of your attendance at a medical school. These expenses are also the most variable. You can cut costs tremendously by living and sharing expenses with other students, for example. I've known of many groups of students who have banded together and rented a house jointly to share the rent and utilities. Not only are your expenses decreased, but you have built-in study mates and companions. Your deep involvement in your studies can often isolate you if you are living alone, leading to loneliness and depression.

Sources of Financial Aid

Now that you understand how your cost of education is determined and what to expect in terms of the cost of a medical education, the second step is to find out what financial aid sources exist and how to apply for them. Financial aid comes from four general sources: the federal government, the state government, the institution itself, and the private sector (e.g., agencies, corporations, associations). Also, there are four types of financial aid: grants, scholarships, loans, and employment. All this, of course, does not include your own personal savings and help from parents or other relatives.

You can figure out your personal financial need by simple mathematics. Once you have computed your total cost of one year of medical education, you then figure out how much money you personally have (with your family's help). Subtract the second number from the first. For example, your cost of education at Mighty Medical School in Anytown, Anystate comes to $31,000. The amount you can pay is $8,500. That leaves you with a financial need of $22,500. You can fill this need through one or several of the types of financial aid available (grants, scholarships, loans, or employment). Of course, the most desirable way is through grants and scholarships which do not have to be repaid.

Gift Aid

Grants and scholarships are called *gift aid*, which consists of funds given to students free and clear. Grants are usually awarded on the basis of a student's financial need and scholarships are awarded on the basis of a student's academic ability. The more gift aid a student receives to cover educational costs, the less that student will have to borrow and owe upon graduation. The down side is that there are fewer funds available to medical students in the form of gift aid than there are in the form of loans. Also, eligibility requirements for gift aid are much more stringent than they are for loans.

There are currently several federal grant/scholarship programs available to medical students.

The Exceptional Financial Need (EFN) Scholarship, as the name indicates, is almost self-explanatory. A small number of first-year students, with zero financial resources, can be granted full tuition and expenses for one year. These are federally funded, but are allotted through the medical college and are awarded to students who agree to fulfill a primary care residency and practice agreement.

National Medical Fellowship (NMF) Program has fellowships available to African-Americans, Native-Americans, Mexican-Americans, and mainland Puerto Ricans. Eligibility is restricted to applicants from these minority groups who demonstrate some financial need for the funds. The amounts awarded will vary from student to student. These awards are usually quite limited, and are allocated to first- and second-year students on the basis of financial need.

The Financial Assistance for Disadvantaged Health Professions Students (FADHPS) is a grant program administered by the Department of Health and Human Services. The criteria for these awards is the same as for the EFN Scholarship, with the exception that the awards do not have to go to the neediest students. As with the EFN Program, the Department of Health and Human Services determines how much FADHPS funds will be given to each institution to allocate to eligible students. The amount awarded to each student is to cover the student's *direct educational costs*.

Several programs exist that offer grant assistance to students in return for a service obligation upon completion of their medical school program or residency. The National Health Service Corps Scholarship (NHSC) is available to students who agree to practice in a location designated as a high-priority health professions area by the Public Health Service. The student receives a grant covering his direct educational costs as well as a stipend each month for living expenses. Medical students who participate in this program incur one year of obligated service for each year of support, with a minimum of a two-year service obligation. The commitment is most often in a very small rural town or poor urban areas, and lasts approximately four years. The Army, Navy, and Air Force also offer grant assistance programs to medical students who agree to serve one year for each year of assistance. Students receive a grant covering their tuition, fees, books, and supplies, as well as a monthly stipend for living expenses. I know of many students who have been supported by these programs. Some are delighted with their assignments (one student was to spend four years in Hawaii). On the other hand, some have been very unhappy and have opted to *buy out* their contracts and have paid heavily in order to practice where they wanted to.

Besides federal grant money, medical schools themselves often offer grant and/or scholarships to selected students. These are usually extremely competitive, offered only to the brightest or neediest students. Once you have decided on the school you will attend, you need to contact the financial aid office or the admissions office to inquire about any programs offered, and how and when to apply for them. As a general rule, more gift aid is available to students who attend a private medical school. This helps to offset the higher tuition charged by the private institutions.

The private sector is the most elusive source of financial assistance. Although hard to come by, the assistance is usually considerable if you are one of the lucky ones to obtain this type of funding. Information about these sources of money can be found through the financial aid office. Sometimes the information is provided through special publications, student newsletters, on bulletin boards, and even on the Internet!

Scholarships and grants are great, but let's face it, not every student will be eligible for this type of funding. The majority of medical students help finance their education through low-interest student loans.

Loans

The one certainty in the world of financial aid is that it will change. The information provided in this section as it relates to federal loans may change by the time this book is published. However, the basic information concerning the types of loans, deferments, interest rates, and maximum loan amounts per year will be helpful in assisting you with your financial planning.

The most common sources of financial aid are government-backed loans. These include:

- Stafford Loans (subsidized and unsubsidized)

- Federal Perkins Loans

- Health Education Assistance Loans (HEAL)

- Primary Care Loans (PCL)

- Supplemental Loans for Students (SLS)

Federal Stafford Loans (subsidized) are awarded on the basis of financial need. The most you can borrow through this program is $8,500 per year; interest rates are capped at 8.25 percent. The interest on this type of loan does not begin to accrue until after you graduate from medical school. The unsubsidized Federal Stafford Loan has the same interest rate, but interest begins to accrue when the loan is dispersed. The annual maximum is $10,000.

The Federal Perkins Loans are issued on the basis of financial need. The maximum amount of funding available is $18,000. These are great loans to get if you are able, as the interest rate is lower than many of the other loans available. The current interest rate is 5 percent. Interest does not begin to accumulate until after medical school graduation. Payments may be deferred for two years of residency.

The Primary Care Loan (PCL) are awarded to students with financial need who agree to complete a primary care residency. There is no specialized limit on the amount borrowed. Instead the limit is a particular school's tuition plus $2,500. Interest rates are currently at 9 percent, with interest accruing only after you begin your repayment schedule. Loan deferments for your entire residency may be available.

Health Education Assistance Loans, or HEAL Loans, are available to most students. Interest begins to accumulate as soon as the money is borrowed. Loan repayment may not begin until your residency is completed. However the interest rate varies quarterly as the 91–day Treasury bill rate plus approximately 2.5 percent.

Other loans include the Loans for Disadvantaged Students (LDS) and private alternative loans available to medical students on the basis of their credit worthiness.

Employment

An additional source of income can be a job. Some medical students have been trained in other fields and have worked as nurses, pharmacists, musicians, or dental hygienists, for example. They are lucky in that they can go back and work a limited amount of hours in their field of training and make a good hourly wage. Other sources of employment can come through other professionals at the medical school. There are many Ph.D.s who are working in specific areas of research who have money for lab assistants through grants. This can be a good source of income and has the plus of developing new skills, as well as looking great on your curriculum vitae when you are applying for residency programs. Certain physicians may also be conducting research in a more clinical setting, instead of basic sciences. There are fewer of these positions and they are well-sought after. Each medical school also may have federal money set aside for what is called a *work–study program*. Work–study programs are another great source of income while going to school and these positions are very popular. You are usually working in a student-related office such as student affairs, admissions, or registrar, or the medical school library, or even as a hall monitor where you can study while doing your job. Students usually limit the amount of time they work in order to maintain studies.

Managing Your Debt

It is very tempting to borrow more and more money. People get tired of living as starving students, which literally they are! Students never miss a free lunch, even if it means sitting through an hour and a half of a real sleeper of a seminar. They hunt down bars with free appetizers and scrounge around for leftover pizza from a faculty noon meeting. Although amusing, this does get tiring after a while. (I know from experience!) But you must remember how essential it is to learn how to delay gratification. Your starving-student status is only temporary. Four years goes quickly, and you'll soon be bringing home a paycheck once you have begun your residency training.

Here are some simple suggestions for controlling your debt:

- Borrow only what you absolutely, positively need.

- Share expenses when possible.

- Learn ways to decrease your utilities (ie., call collect and lower your thermostat significantly).

- Learn the bargain places to shop.

- Clip coupons.

- Date a person with a job.

- Pray.

According to the 1993 American Association of Medical College Graduate Questionnaire, these are some of the statistics of student debt:

- One half of all medical students had debts between $100,000 and $150,000.

- The median medical school debt in 1993 was $50,000.

- The estimated average debt for 1994 is $70,000.

The importance of managing your debt is simple. You must pay back all loans and the payments will, most likely, be large. The more you borrow, the larger your payment will be. Let's use an example.

Laura has borrowed $18,000 through Perkins Loans. This was the maximum money she could obtain from this source. The current rate of interest is 5 percent, and with the number of monthly payments at 120 (ten years), her monthly payment will be $190.93. "Well, that's not so bad," you reply. Oh, but we're not finished yet! Laura also received a Stafford Loan (subsidized) of $8,500 per year for four years. This money totals $34,000 and was borrowed at 8 percent interest. This payback adds $600.55 to Laura's monthly total. So this brings her payment to $791.48 per month. In her third and fourth years, Laura obtained an unsubsidized Stafford Loan at the same interest rate as her subsidized Federal Stafford Loans (8 percent). Since Laura borrowed a total of $10,000 from this program, she has a loan repayment charge of $121.33 for 120 months. Her total debt, then is $62,000, and her monthly payments run approximately $912.81. Laura's debt, while not insignificant, is actually less than that of most of her peers—the estimated median debt for students graduating from medical school in 1994 is over $70,000 and many students have debts of over $100,000. At an interest rate of 8 percent, the monthly payment would be $1213.28! That is a lot of money to part with every month!

So you can see how important it is to keep your debt as low as possible. By borrowing the maximum amount of money available, you will increase your standard of living during medical school. You may drive a sports car and be able to live in a nice condo, but be sure to know that you'll be paying for it with your future earnings!

Another important reason to keep your debt at a minimum is that you do not want your financial situation to determine which field of medicine you pursue. If you are faced with $150,000 worth of debt, you may be forced to choose a more lucrative specialty. Your true desire may be to practice pediatrics in the small town where you grew up. But you may decide it's necessary to go into a surgical specialty, which is not your first love, to reap the benefits of a higher income to support loan repayments. You should never allow money to dictate your life to this extent.

A very important point to know is this: Each medical school will employ a very knowledgeable person to deal with financial aid. Some schools will have their own financial aid counselor whose entire job deals with students and their financial needs. You have just familiarized your self with types of financial assistance. Check the Personal Admissions Planner at the end of the book for a budget page. You can estimate your potential medical school costs and your financial need. Once you have accepted a position in a medical school, seek out counsel from the financial aid advisor to begin your application processes.

Appendix

A Day in the Life of a Physician
by Frank A. Redmond, M.D., Ph.D.

"To know even one life has breathed easier because you have lived; this is to have succeeded." Ralph Waldo Emerson

Writing about the average day in the life of a physician is a daunting task! It is as if I were asked to describe the entire continent of Africa, country by country, or to speak about the taste of every kind of American food. There is simply no "typical day" for any single doctor, let alone a "typical" day for physicians in general.

As an emergency physician, I lead a very different life from that of my colleagues in other specialities. We ER docs have highly variable schedules. Nights, weekends, and all holidays are part of our calendar. Many people have an image of the job of emergency physician from their own encounters with an ER. This view, however, is merely a snapshot of a moment in the daily schedule.

The ER is often filled to capacity with crying children, panicked parents, and men and women in pain. Remember, although the pain each patient feels when entering an ER is real and important, there are many other patients seeking care, all at the same time. All these people think that theirs is the most important case. And of course, that's human. But this is a big part of the frustration that makes up the fabric of an ER doc's life. Everyone is clamoring for your attention. Everyone deserves your attention immediately, but that is impossible. So there is always waiting, and hence, always some complaining.

A day in the ER is so varied that entire books and television series have been based on its scenarios. The fast pace, the varied cases, the many stories that unfold are always fascinating. So let's take a look at a typical afternoon shift.

The Day

3 P.M. to 11 P.M.

If I'm scheduled for the 3 P.M. shift, I'll show up ready to work in the ER at approximately 2:59. In reality, my day will have begun much earlier. By 7 A.M. I am up, awake, and making coffee. Pretty much the same routine as every other working American. I glance at the paper, let the dog out, and maybe do some additional reading. Then it's time to get the kids ready for school, gather homework papers, find lost shoes, and shoo them out the door. A lot of work, and it's not even 9 A.M. yet! Now comes the part that most medical students focus on when considering a career in emergency medicine: I have the rest of the day totally free, right? Wrong! I usually have meetings at the hospital, community work, lunch gatherings, hospital committees, or a whole host of other things to do. Most of these responsibilities more closely resemble work than play. (All this, and we haven't even considered the list of chores at home.) There are a few scattered days in the month, however, where I can schedule eighteen holes of golf, a day with the family, or lunch with friends before the start of my shift.

Okay. So let's assume that I've worked my way through the day until 2:30 P.M. Now it's time to hot foot it down to the hospital. In our department, which has a moderate volume (25,000 patient visits per year), there will be one *attending* physician and one family physician on duty.

The attending is a physician who is in charge at any given time. He or she has completed a medical residency program. In the case of the ER, the attending physician has completed a 3 or 4 year residency program in the specialty of emergency medicine. You may encounter many other types of attending physicians during your medical school career.

So, it is now 3 P.M. and I am ready to relieve the attending physician. She will have been on duty since 7 A.M., and during that time will have seen 20 to 30 patients. If it has been a busy day, she may have a few patients to *hand over*. These are those patients that the first-shift doctor cannot finish up with before going home. Many departments, including ours have the luxury of what's called *second coverage*. This consists of a second doctor present in the department during peak hours to help with the patient flow. We often have a family physician for this task, although other departments may use paramedics, physician's assistants, residents, or other emergency physicians. The second doc will have picked up most of the new patients since 2 P.M.,which usually allows for a minimal number of patients to be transferred to me. These hold-overs are most likely patients who have complicated problems or are waiting for extensive lab work.

The first half hour of any shift is usually not too hectic, so I can grab a cup of coffee, check the mail, or get a stack of charts to dictate. If the department is already busy, I'll dive right in and start seeing patients. Included in the general mayhem of masses of patients are residents and medical students. In a teaching institution like ours, it is unusual for me to see patients by myself. At my side I normally have someone who is learning. In addition to all the medical students, residents, attending and second-coverage docs, there are the usual number of nurses, ward clerks, transcriptionists, radiology techs, and a host of others. If there are patients to be admitted to other departments, such as pediatrics or surgery, there may also be residents and students from that service as well. This all combines into what looks and sounds like utter chaos to most people. But I love these sights and sounds. This is what gets my heart pumping and my senses peaked for performance. This is why I chose the specialty of emergency medicine!

What will we see during this shift? Only the passage of eight hours till the end of the shift will tell. There's a woman with abdominal pain in room 4, a young boy with a cut chin, a man with torn fingers from a factory accident, a street person with a drug overdose. There are as many different stories as there are patients. What seems like a never ending stream of people is due to the fact that our doors are never closed. There is never an end to people seeking care in our emergency department. To be sure, there are times that are quiet; times that the pulse of the ER slows way down. These, too, are cherished moments that give us time to catch up on reading, dictating, or just talking with our fellow team-members. How's your new baby doing? Where are you going for your next vacation? Did you hear the latest news about the hospital?...

Sometimes 11 P.M. rolls around in the blink of an eye. The fast pace and the sheer number of patients lead to the quick passage of time. I glance up at the clock to see that the shift is nearly over. Another day without dinner—no wonder my stomach's been howling! That patient with the acute MI (heart attack) just didn't allow for a dinner break tonight. Maybe tomorrow will be slower. I wash up, change out of my scrubs, and check for some final lab reports on several of my last patients. I'd rather stay a few minutes over and finish up, rather than hand over my patients. I always like to complete the job I started. There may be one or two that just can't be finalized, such as the elderly gentleman waiting for a CAT scan he needs due to a head injury, and the little girl waiting for the results of some blood tests. Eureka! There's my replacement now! I'll head on home.

Unwinding

The house is dark when I pull into the drive, all except the kitchen light left on for me by my wife. If the kids haven't eaten all of the dinner, there may even be a place still set for me at the table. The plate with plastic wrap covering the now-cold lasagna is ready for the microwave. It tastes incredibly good and makes me feel welcome and grateful to have such a healthy family. Many of the patients I saw today have never experienced much love or warmth. It is easy to bring them home with me (in my mind). Particularly the kids. The baby who died from SIDS. The beautiful blonde, blue-eyed two-year-old boy who choked to death on a piece of apple (which his mom had cut up into tiny pieces so he wouldn't choke!). The dark-haired little girl just diagnosed with leukemia. The poor little five-year-old who died of massive head injuries because the dad didn't bother with seat belts! The list can go on and on.... I have to fight this tendency to relive some of the horrors. However, the longer I'm in practice, the easier it gets.

I have a wind-down routine. It has grown shorter as the years go by. If I want to get a good night's sleep, I know it is a must to clear my mind. I'll probably watch a few minutes of "Late Night with David Letterman" or CNN and be asleep in bed by midnight. One of the job skills we learn as physicians is to put our minds at ease and get rest whenever we are able. Who knows when the phone will ring and off we'll have to go again?

The Realities of Medicine

What, you may ask, about other specialities? Are all doctor's lives so crazy? The simple answer is "Yes" We are all a bunch of sleep-deprived maniacs at times.

People who hold jobs in other fields remark about this. For example, we have a program at our local (county) medical society called a mini-internship. This is a two-day event in which a business person or politician follows a doctor for one day. The second day he or she then switches to another doctor. The universal comment from the participants is how amazingly difficult a doctor's day is, especially from a physicial standpoint. We doctors don't always realize how physically demanding is our profession. Many of us are literally on our feet all day long.

Apart from the fairly intense physical activity, what about other doctors' lives? These are extremely variable. For example, the pathologist may have a fairly regular schedule. The family physician in solo practice may not take a single vacation for many years and literally be on call twenty-four hours a day. A fourteen-hour day may be the norm for a vascular surgeon. One psychiatrist may work part-time, while another puts in many grueling days in a row. There is no such thing as a typical day for any physician! Especially in the 1990s, doctors' lives have never been so varied. For instance, I have recently changed jobs to become a physician–administrator. I have become a vice president for medical affairs for my hospital. This is a position that didn't even exist until the last few years. A "VPMA," as we are called, is basically a liaison between the hospital and the doctors. We are called upon to help facilitate the smooth interaction between the business of the hospital and the business of the physicians. Reimbursement (pay), quality of care, continuing medical education, and government interactions are all in a day's work for me now. So here is an entirely new area in which a doctor can become involved—hospital administration.

Keeping Current and Moving Ahead

An important part of any physician's work is continuing medical education, or CME. CME is the education we physicians must participate in each year following graduation from residency. Each state has specific requirements for the amount of classroom work that must be undertaken each year.

Most states require approximately 50 hours per year of continuing education. Some of this must be in the formal setting of a lecture-type format, while other credits may be gained from reading materials and then submitting a self-administered test. Either way, CME can seem like a hassle, but is very important in order to maintain our high standards of patient care. Medicine is constantly moving ahead. Each physician has a responsibility to self, patients, and community to keep abreast of all the latest medical findings. After fifteen years of practice, it is possible—and human—to forget some of the medical education of the past! So CME is a means of relearning as well.

Then there are the journals. I get six or seven different journals a month. Some are freebies sent by companies, others are magazines sent by professional societies. Either way, it all adds up to a lot of mail to be sorted, and more reading to be added to an already crammed schedule. All this, and we haven't even talked about reading for pleasure—a must in order to remain sane in this chaotic world!

Would I Do It Over?

Absolutely, 100 percent, no hesitation, "Yes!"

Medicine is a noble profession. It is an honor to be a physician. Although the hours are long and grueling, the work sometimes smelly and tiresome, the threat of lawyers constantly hangs over your every move, I would never choose another profession. It is an overwhelming privilege to be a physician. To help just one human being enjoy a healthier, more productive life, to save the life of just one child, to ease the pain of just one dying patient makes the long road of education well worth the trip.

Perhaps to some, medicine is just a job like any other. You can view it as toil, labor. You can see the work as just another way to put bread on the table. But for many of us, the ones who truly believe in what the field of medicine is all about, the actual practice of medicine becomes a transforming, almost religious experience. The ability to put *self* aside and concentrate on helping others is one of the greatest human gifts. Medicine offers a wonderful opportunity to put that gift to use.

Personal Admissions Planner

What is the
Personal Admissions Planner?

This section of the book is designed for your personal notes, comments, and evaluations. It is time for you to start a file to keep track of all your past records and your future grades, MCAT scores, and other paper work. You can also keep a record of your required courses, professors, and grades. You should begin to get into the habit of making copies of *everything*. When you receive your grade reports, make a copy. When your MCAT scores are sent to you, make a copy. It doesn't hurt to make a copy of any correspondence between you and a medical school. Take these copies and put them into a file, then file the folder away in a safe place. When you begin applying to medical schools, you can pick up your folder and you have all your needed information right in front of you. Believe me, you can't get organized too soon.

It is also to your benefit to start a journal. Keep accounts of jobs, volunteer work, hobbies, and projects. Make notes concerning coursework and grades occasionally. Perhaps you missed an A by only two points. Or the highest grade in the course was a B, and you got it! You think you'll never forget these points, but you will. So jot them down! You can also list non-required, but advantageous, courses to take. In this way, you can be aware at all times where you stand in your course work.

There are worksheets for keeping track of personal mentors, high school teachers, physicians, and others who can be contacted for advice, letters, and other help. Other worksheets can be used to keep your own list of schools to contact, application deadlines, and the status of correspondence. There are worksheets to be used for individualized self-evaluation so you can determine the best qualities to emphasize about yourself on applications. An additional group of pages will be used for all of your interview information. It is very important to keep track of interview dates and your impressions of the medical schools you visit. Use "The Waiting List" to keep track of acceptances and rejections and your replies. There will also be a worksheet devoted to the actual application process, with pages for composing a personal statement, a list of people to contact for letters of recommendation, and a timetable of important deadlines.

SO YOU WANT TO BE A DOCTOR?

Here is a checklist of questions you should ask yourself. Put a check next to the statements that you feel are true about yourself.

✓ 1. I like working with people.
✓ 2. I am a team player.
✓ 3. I enjoy reading.
✓ 4. I live a healthy lifestyle.
✓ 5. I am focused.
✓ 6. I can be selfless.
✓ 7. I enjoy helping people. It helps me feel good about myself.
✓ 8. I have integrity.
✓ 9. I am able to make personal sacrifices.
✓ 10. I am able to delay gratification.
✓ 11. I am dedicated.
✓ 12. I am able to evaluate myself honestly.
✓ 13. I am caring and compassionate.
✓ 14. I always liked school.
✓ 15. Science was always one of my favorite subjects.
✓ 16. I am not afraid of criticism.
✓ 17. I like laboratory courses.
✓ 18. I have good communication skills.
✓ 19. I have previously made commitments and have honored them.
✓ 20. I have high moral and ethical standards.
✓ 21. I am honest and reliable.
___ 22. I can cope with stress and high anxiety levels.
✓ 23. I am a hard worker.
___ 24. I have good time-management skills.
✓ 25. I have a good memory.
___ 26. I can handle failure.
✓ 27. I have previously set goals and have achieved them.
___ 28. I am a self-starter.
✓ 29. I am able to work on my own with little guidance.
___ 30. I am basically a positive person.
✓ 31. I understand some of the basic problems that plague medicine today.
✓ 32. I feel I have a lot to offer in my career choice.
✓ 33. A career in which I find satisfaction and enjoy is more important to me than the monetary rewards.
✓ 34. I feel excited when I think about medical school and life as a doctor.
✓ 35. I love challenges.

Add up the total number of checks, and use the scoring information below to interpret your results.

33–35: You definitely have the qualities necessary to pursue a career in medicine.

30–32: You have the basic characteristics needed for a career in medicine. Continue to strengthen your personal attributes and work on the negatives.

27–29: Medicine is a possible career option, but you need to work on your weak points and turn them into positives.

26 and below: You need to reevaluate your career choice.

HIGH SCHOOL ACHIEVEMENTS

Basic Information:

Class Rank _____   ACT scores _____

GPA _____   SAT scores _____

SGPA _____   Other _____

Awards:

Extracurricular Activities:

Work Experience:

Volunteer Work:

THE COLLEGE YEARS

1. Coursework
   Required Courses for *Most* Medical Schools:
   __ Biology (1 full year)   Grade_A B____
   __ General Chemistry (1 full year)   Grade_A B____
   __ Organic Chemistry (1 full year)   Grade_B____
   __ Physics (1 full year)   Grade_A____
   __ English (1 full year)   Grade_A A____

   Required Courses for *Many* Medical Schools:
   __ Mathematics (1 full year)   Grade_____
   __ Calculus   Grade_B____
   __ Psychology   Grade_A____
   __ Social Sciences   Grade_____
   __ Statistics   Grade_A____

   Required Courses for *Some* Medical Schools:
   __ Analytical Chemistry   Grade_____
   __ Genetics   Grade_____
   __ Physical Chemistry   Grade_____
   __ Foreign Language   Grade_A____

   Additional Courses that Will Help You in Medical School:
   __ Vertebrate Anatomy   Grade_____
   __ Histology   Grade_____
   __ Embryology   Grade_____
   __ Molecular Biology   Grade_____
   __ Physiology   Grade_____
   __ Biochemistry   Grade_____

   Explanations of Any Courses or Grades:

2. Extracurricular Activities:

   Campus Leadership Roles:

Campus Organizations:

Volunteer/Philanthropic Activities:

Work Experience:

Hospital Experience:

3. Future References:

Professor	Course	Grade
1.		
2.		
3.		
4.		
5.		

Pre-Medical Advisor:

Deans or Administrators:

Work Employers/Bosses:

Coaches/Group Leaders:

Registrar (for future transcripts):

Personal Mentors:

4. Developing People Skills
    One of the unwritten requirements for medical schools is having good
    people skills. Here are some suggestions for developing these qualities:
    Coursework:
    __ Public Speaking   Grade_____
    __ Communication   Grade_____
    __ Theater/Drama   Grade_ A____
    Working with People:

    Employment:
    __ Leader/boss
    Volunteer work:
    __ Drama
    __ Speaking to groups on behalf of organizations such as American
       Heart Association, American Cancer Society, Smoking Cessation,
       etc.
    Extracurricular Activities:
    __ Sports
    __ Leadership Roles
    __ Theater
    __ Debate
    __ Publications/Writing
    Hospital Experience:

    Team Efforts:
    __ Sports
    __ Community Projects
    __ Other
    Traveling:
    __ U.S.
    __ Abroad
    __ Foreign Study

POST-GRADUATE EXPERIENCES

Many of you who are applying to medical school have been out of school for one or more years. This can often be a plus for you. It is important to emphasize your growth and maturity during your years following graduation from a college or university.

What have you done since graduation from college?

1. Graduate School:

    Courses:

    Degree Earned:

2. Jobs and/or Careers:

3. Travel:

4. Volunteer Work:

MEDICAL COLLEGE ADMISSION TEST

Prepare to take the MCAT in the SPRING of your JUNIOR YEAR in college.

A. Preparations:

    __ Pick up application packet for the MCAT.

    __ Check date of test.

    __ Fill out application for the exam.

    __ Send application well before the deadline (usually 2 months prior to date of exam).

    Be sure to include:

    __ 1. The candidate information folder

    __ 2. The signed identification card with a current passport-type picture

    __ 3. The registration fee

    __ Mark the test date on your calendar.

    __ Once you receive your test center admission ticket, put it in a safe place.

B. On the date of testing, remember to bring with you:

    __ 1. Admission ticket

    __ 2. Official personal identification which has a photo

    __ 3. Three (number 2) soft-lead pencils

    __ 4. An eraser

    __ 5. Two ballpoint pens (black ink) for the writing sample

    __ 6. A watch to help you keep track of time

C. Results of the MCAT:

    VERBAL REASONING   _____

    PHYSICAL SCIENCES   _____

    WRITING SAMPLE   _____

    BIOLOGICAL SCIENCES _____

D. Send results to:
    1.

    2.

    3.

    4.

    5.

AMCAS APPLICATION PROCESS

I. THE APPLICATION

The most important points about your application are these:

Be Neat

Be Honest

Be Complete

Never Miss a Deadline!

The Earlier the Better!

AMCAS begins accepting applications on June 15. KEEP THIS DATE IN MIND.

II. THE PERSONAL STATEMENT

Begin by thinking about what you want to include in this very important part of your application. Write down your main points in an outline form. Don't just reiterate what is on your application. Tell a story. Describe a turning point in your life. Why did you choose medicine? What unique qualities do you possess? How have school, family, work, and extracurricular activities helped develop who you are and your personal qualities? You can begin this process now by using the space provided to jot down your ideas.

Personal Statement

III. TRANSCRIPTS

In February of your junior year, begin contacting the registrars of all the schools you have attended. Request that your transcripts be sent to:

> AMCAS
> Section for Student Services
> Association of American Medical Colleges
> 2450 N. Street., N. W., Suite 201
> Washington D. C. 20037-1131

At the same time, request a personal copy of your transcripts. You can use these transcripts for filling out your application. You can also photocopy the transcripts to give to possible references, so that they can look over your academic record.

Remember, AMCAS begins accepting transcripts on March 15. Don't wait until the last minute. Also, have all updates sent to AMCAS following completion of all your courses at the end of your senior year.

IV. LETTERS OF RECOMMENDATION

Following the MCAT exam, you should begin to contact all the people who might write a letter of recommendation for you. Although these letters aren't a part of the actual AMCAS application, they are very important! Steps to Follow:

1. Carefully choose the people whom you ask to write your letters of recommendation. Be sure they know you!
2. Contact each individual personally.
3. Give each individual copies of your transcripts, MCAT scores (when you receive them), and a brief description of your hobbies, interests, extracurricular activities, leadership roles, community service, volunteer work, work experience, and any other pertinent information. This is very useful for the writers to review.
4. Give each writer a specific date to have the letter written and sent. These letters are NOT a part of the application itself. AMCAS begins accepting applications on June 1.

V. APPLICATION CHECKLIST:

__ 1. Fill out all portions of the application, using a typewriter or word processor.
__ 2. Prepare the personal statement.
__ 3. Have an English professor and/or another faculty member or friend read it and make comments.
__ 4. Contact registrar from ALL schools attended and have transcripts sent to AMCAS.
__ 5. Contact all writers of letters of recommendation and provide them with all your information.
__ 6. Include AMCAS application fee with application.

NON-AMCAS SCHOOLS

The procedure is slightly different for applying to non-AMCAS schools. There is no central application processing center. You must contact each school individually, request an application, and follow its individual application procedures and deadlines.

CHECKLIST:

__ 1. Request application for each non-AMCAS school.
__ 2. Fill out each application.
__ 3. Have all transcripts sent to each school.
__ 4. Send in each school's application fee.
__ 5. Have MCAT scores sent to each school.
__ 6. Follow any additional requests or instructions for each school.
__ 7. Provide all people who will write letters of recommendation with all needed materials including the addresses of all non-AMCAS schools to which you are applying.

THE INTERVIEW PROCESS

A. PREPARING FOR THE INTERVIEW

Ask yourself these questions:

1. Why have I chosen medicine as a career?
2. Why would I make a good doctor?
3. Do I know what a physician does on a day-to-day basis?
4. Do I have a special interest in a medical specialty? If so, what and why?
5. What are my best qualities?
6. What is my greatest weakness? How do I try to improve on that weakness?

B. LIST OF SCHOOLS THAT HAVE INVITED YOU FOR AN INTERVIEW

Name	Location	Interview date
1.		
2.		
3.		
4.		
5.		
6.		
7.		

C. INTERVIEW CHECKLIST

__ 1. Have I done some research on the school?
__ 2. Do I have travel plans coordinated with the school?
__ 3. Do I need overnight accommodations?
__ 4. Have I reviewed my grades, MCAT scores, application, and personal statement?
__ 5. Have I practiced my interviewing skills?
__ 6. Do I have appropriate clothes? Haircut?
__ 7. Have I kept up with current events and trends in medicine?

D. AFTER EACH INTERVIEW ASK YOURSELF THESE QUESTIONS:

1. Was I on time?
2. Was I honest?
3. Did I speak articulately, or was I stumbling and searching for words?
4. Did my interviewer(s) get to know me?
5. Did I feel reasonably comfortable?

6. Did I like my interviewer(s)? Students? Faculty? Support Staff? Administrators?
7. Did I send a thank-you note to the appropriate people?
8. What did I learn from this interview?

Ask yourself these questions following each and every interview. Your first interview will definitely be a learning experience. Each subsequent interview will go a bit more easily, and you will be more confident. So if you can arrange it, pick the school you are least interested in for your first interview experience.

YOUR PERSONAL LIST

Following your final interview, rank the schools in the order of your preference. Begin with your number-one choice. Then keep track of the responses you receive.

School	Accepted	Rejected	Wait listed
1.			
2.			
3.			
4.			
5.			
6.			
7.			

Jot down the date you receive your letter. *Respond immediately*! If you are accepted to a school and haven't yet made your decision, be courteous and respond appropriately. You usually have two weeks to reply.

RULES TO FOLLOW DURING THE ACCEPTANCE PROCESS

1. Always respond promptly to any correspondence.
2. If you telephone your response, follow with a letter.
3. You can hold no more than ONE acceptance at a time.
4. When you've made your final acceptance decision, promptly withdraw your application from all other schools.

POINTS TO REMEMBER CONCERNING ACCEPTANCES

1. Medical schools that use a rolling admissions system begin accepting students as early as October 15.
2. Many schools release ALL their acceptance letters on March 15.
3. Most schools will refund your acceptance deposit until May 15.
4. After May 15, medical schools begin to actively seek responses and are free to contact you, if you have not yet answered them, and request a decision.

COMPLETE CHECKLIST OF DATES

Junior Year (or the year prior to applying to medical school):

__ FEBRUARY
- Obtain application packet for the Spring MCAT.
- Check date of MCAT and mark the date!

__ MARCH 15
- AMCAS begins accepting transcripts.

__ APRIL
- Spring MCAT given.
- Obtain AMCAS Application from AMCAS or premedical counselor.

__ JUNE 15
- AMCAS begins accepting applications.
- You'll probably receive your MCAT scores sometime this month.

__ JULY
- If you plan to retake the MACT or had decided to put it off, be sure to check on the date of the September testing. Obtain your application for the exam and send it in.

Senior year (applying and interviewing):

__ SEPTEMBER
- FALL MCAT. Be sure to have your scores sent to all the schools to which you are applying.
- Be sure to have your AMCAS application in! Remember, the earlier the better—some students are already in the process of interviewing.
- Begin keeping track of schools requesting supplemental applications. See end of checklist.

OCTOBER
- The EARLIEST date that a school with a rolling admissions policy will offer an acceptance.

OCTOBER through FEBRUARY
- INTERVIEWS
  Keep track of all interviews, dates, and impressions.

MARCH 15
- All letters of acceptance are released.

MAY 15
- Medical schools are free to contact you if you have not yet responded.

MAY 15 through AUGUST (or date classes begin)
- Medical schools continue to offer acceptance to applicants on waiting lists.

AUGUST/SEPTEMBER
- Medical school classes begin. Very occasionally, a medical school will have an opening following the beginning of classes. If you are on a waiting list, let the school know you can be there in a moment's notice (if you can !).

Supplemental applications:
Following the initial review of a person's application, some schools request a supplemental application. This is usually an additional set of questions for you to answer. At the same time a supplemental form is requested, the school will ask for your letters of recommendation. Begin keeping track of which schools request your letters of recommendation and a supplemental application.

School	Supplemental Application Requested	Date Sent
1.		
2.		
3.		
4.		
5.		

HERE'S LOOKING AT YOU, KID!

SELF-ASSESSMENT:

Let's take a look and you and your application through the eyes of an admissions committee member. The five main questions an admission committee member will be asking concerning YOU are:

1. Can you make it through four years of medical school?

List 5 points that demonstrate you can.

1)

2)

3)

4)

5)

2. Do you show sufficient motivation for a career in medicine?

List 3 areas in your life that show motivation.

1)

2)

3)

List 3 ways you can demonstrate your interest in the medical field.

1)

2)

3)

3. Are you committed to many years of difficult schooling and training?

List several ways in which you've spent time in pursuing your goals.

1)

2)

3)

List two ways in which you have had to delay gratification in order to meet a specific goal or challenge:

1)

2)

4. Will you make a caring physician?

Give several examples of incidences where you have exhibited compassion or empathy.

1)

2)

3)

5. Did you show interest in the school?
How?

1)

2)

3)

WORKING OUT A BUDGET

Finding ways to finance your medical education can be a real challenge. The first step is to work out a budget and determine how much money you have, and how much you need to finance through gifts, loans, or scholarships.

1. Let's determine the <u>DIRECT COSTS</u>:

TUITION   _____
GENERAL FEES   _____
COURSE FEES   _____
INSURANCE   _____
IMMUNIZATIONS   _____
    SUBTOTAL 1   _____

If you know which school you will be attending, great. If not, choose the most expensive school to work out the maximum money you will need to attend the first year.

<u>INDIRECT COSTS</u>:

RENT   _____
UTILITIES   _____
FOOD   _____
PERSONAL   _____
BOOKS/SUPPLIES   _____
TRANSPORTATION   _____
    SUBTOTAL 2   _____

Now add Subtotal 1 and 2 together:

SUBTOTAL 1   _____
SUBTOTAL 2   _____
    GRAND TOTAL   _____

2. Now you know how much money you need for your first year. Your second step is to determine how much money you have saved, money you may borrow from friends or family members, and money you may receive as a scholarship. Add this all up for YOUR MONEY: _____

Now subtract YOUR MONEY from the GRAND TOTAL:

GRAND TOTAL   _____
    (minus)
YOUR MONEY   –   _____
    MONEY NEEDED   _____

The MONEY NEEDED, _____ , is the money you will need to finance through loans.

You can bring this information with you to the financial aid counselor who will help you determine the best ways for you to finance the balance of money needed.

VGM CAREER BOOKS

CAREER DIRECTORIES
Careers Encyclopedia
Dictionary of Occupational Titles
Occupational Outlook Handbook

CAREERS FOR
Animal Lovers
Bookworms
Caring People
Computer Buffs
Crafty People
Culture Lovers
Environmental Types
Fashion Plates
Film Buffs
Foreign Language Aficionados
Good Samaritans
Gourmets
Health Nuts
History Buffs
Kids at Heart
Nature Lovers
Night Owls
Number Crunchers
Plant Lovers
Shutterbugs
Sports Nuts
Travel Buffs
Writers

CAREERS IN
Accounting; Advertising; Business;
Child Care; Communications;
Computers; Education;
Engineering;
the Environment; Finance;
Government; Health Care; High
Tech; International Business;
Journalism; Law; Marketing;
Medicine; Science; Social &
Rehabilitation Services

CAREER PLANNING
Beating Job Burnout
Beginning Entrepreneur
Career Planning & Development for
College Students &
Recent Graduates
Career Change
Careers Checklists
College and Career Success for
Students with Learning Disabilities
Complete Guide to Career Etiquette
Cover Letters They Don't Forget
Dr. Job's Complete Career Guide
Executive Job Search Strategies

Guide to Basic Cover Letter
Writing
Guide to Basic Résumé Writing
Guide to Internet Job Searching
Guide to Temporary Employment
Job Interviewing for College
Students
Joyce Lain Kennedy's Career Book
Out of Uniform
Slam Dunk Résumés
The Parent's Crash Course in
Career Planning: Helping Your
College Student Succeed

CAREER PORTRAITS
Animals; Cars; Computers;
Electronics; Fashion;
Firefighting; Music; Nursing;
Sports; Teaching; Travel; Writing

GREAT JOBS FOR
Business Majors
Communications Majors
Engineering Majors
English Majors
Foreign Language Majors
History Majors
Psychology Majors

HOW TO
Apply to American Colleges and
Universities
Approach an Advertising Agency and
Walk Away with the Job You Want
Be a Super Sitter
Bounce Back Quickly After
Losing Your Job
Change Your Career
Choose the Right Career
Cómo escribir un currículum vitae
en inglés que tenga éxito
Find Your New Career Upon
Retirement
Get & Keep Your First Job
Get Hired Today
Get into the Right Business School
Get into the Right Law School
Get into the Right Medical School
Get People to Do Things Your Way
Have a Winning Job Interview
Hit the Ground Running in Your
New Job
Hold It All Together When You've
Lost Your Job
Improve Your Study Skills
Jumpstart a Stalled Career

Land a Better Job
Launch Your Career in TV News
Make the Right Career Moves
Market Your College Degree
Move from College into a
Secure Job
Negotiate the Raise You Deserve
Prepare Your Curriculum Vitae
Prepare for College
Run Your Own Home Business
Succeed in Advertising When all
You Have Is Talent
Succeed in College
Succeed in High School
Take Charge of Your Child's Early
Education
Write a Winning Résumé
Write Successful Cover Letters
Write Term Papers & Reports
Write Your College Application Essay

MADE EASY
Cover Letters
Getting a Raise
Job Hunting
Job Interviews
Résumés

OPPORTUNITIES IN
This extensive series provides
detailed information on nearly 150
individual career fields.

RÉSUMÉS FOR
Advertising Careers
Architecture and Related Careers
Banking and Financial Careers
Business Management Careers
College Students &
Recent Graduates
Communications Careers
Education Careers
Engineering Careers
Environmental Careers
Ex-Military Personnel
50+ Job Hunters
Government Careers
Health and Medical Careers
High School Graduates
High Tech Careers
Law Careers
Midcareer Job Changes
Re-Entering the Job Market
Sales and Marketing Careers
Scientific and Technical Careers
Social Service Careers
The First-Time Job Hunter

 VGM Career Horizons
a division of *NTC Publishing Group*
4255 West Touhy Avenue
Lincolnwood, Illinois 60646–1975